EDIBLE PLANTS

An inspirational guide to choosing and growing unusual edible plants

Contents

1.	The Plants for a Future Concept	03
2.	Alternative Food Crops	05
3.	Alternative Fruits	09
4.	Alternative Root Crops	15
5.	Alternative Edible Leaves	21
6.	Edible Flowers	28
7.	Winter Salads	34
8.	Staple Seed Crops from Perennials	39
9.	Vegetable Oils	43
10.	Fruit - Food of the Gods	46
11.	Green Gold - The Leaves of Life!	50
12.	Useful Weeds	53
13.	Annuals in the Perennial Garden	60
14.	Index	70

Introduction: The Plants for a Future Concept

This book provides information on unusual edible plants that can be grown in Britain (or in similar climatic conditions elsewhere). Its contents have been derived from entries in the Plants For A Future (PFAF) database, which is available via the internet at www.pfaf.org. The database was originally created twenty years ago to document the knowledge gained from the practical project carried out from 1989 by Ken and Addy Fern at their experimental site in Cornwall. The Ferns carried out research and provided information on edible and otherwise useful plants suitable for growing outdoors in a temperate climate, and eventually grew 1,500 species at the site. Many of the findings and recommendations herein are the results of their work. (Most of the planting, observation and testing at the Cornwall site took place during the 1990s. In order to maximise the knowledge that can be gleaned from the project, in 2009 the PFAF charity commissioned a detailed study and mapping of the then current state of the site. The report from that study is available via the website.)

The PFAF database now includes information on approximately 7,000 useful plants. It is administered by the PFAF charity, which was originally set up to support the Ferns research and educational work, but is now largely restricted to maintaining and improving the Plants database, and continuing to make it freely available.

It is evident that plants can provide us with the majority of our needs, and in a way that cares for the health of the planet. A wide range of plants can be grown to meet all our food needs and many other commodities, whilst also providing a diversity of habitats for native flora and fauna. With a rapidly growing global population and increasingly unpredictable climate, food security has become a serious concern. There are over 20,000 species of edible plants known in the world, yet fewer than 20 species now provide 90% of our food. Large areas of land devoted to single crops increase dependence upon the intervention of chemicals and intensive control methods, with the added threat of soil depletion and the development of chemical-resistant insects and new diseases. More diversity of crops is urgently needed, and some of the lesser known plants in this book may have a useful part to play in future food production systems.

It is interesting to compare a large-scale intensively cultivated field to an equivalent area of natural woodland. The woodland receives little or no intervention but produces lush growth and a diversity of plants and animals. The cultivated land supports very few species. The quality and depth of soil in a woodland is maintained and improved by natural processes, but in contrast cultivated fields often suffer from erosion and loss of soil structure, and require costly agro-chemical inputs to remain productive.

We seek to encourage the cultivation of perennial plants, together with some self-seeding annuals. A large part of the reason for this is the difference in the amount of time and energy it takes to cultivate and harvest crops. Annuals means the cultivation of the ground every year, sowing the seeds, controlling the weeds, adding fertilizers and attempting to control pests and diseases. It all seems so much extra work compared to planting and establishing a perennial, and then waiting to harvest its yield.

Not only do people seem trapped in a method of growing with lower yields for far more input, but also one that is damaging the environment, and all the plants and animals that live in it.

Continued intensive cultivation not only creates a hostile environment for most of our wild plants and animals, but it also destroys the organic matter in the soil and opens it up to the risk of erosion from wind and rain. The soil structure is damaged and tends to becomes compacted, leaving it unable to drain properly or allow plant roots to penetrate and obtain nutrients, and valuable topsoil is washed away in heavy rain.

A cultivated crop such as wheat has all its roots in a narrow band of soil, with intense competition between plants for the same nutrients. Any nutrients below this level are inaccessible to the plants. Each crop plant is susceptible to the same pests and diseases and has similar climatic requirements; if one plant suffers they all suffer. The amount of energy used in producing high yields is often far more than the food itself yields in energy. This is simply not sustainable.

Another valuable approach is Woodland Gardening, where the design seeks to emulate beneficial aspects of natural woodland. In woodland trees and plants continue to grow year after year and habitats are provided for a host of animals. But almost no weeding is required, no feeding and no watering. A wide range of plants can grow side by side each occupying its own space; some with deep roots bringing up nutrients from beyond the reach of others. When leaves fall they provide nutrients and substance to the soil. Plants with shallow root systems obtain their nutrients from nearer the surface of the soil. The canopy of trees creates a shelter and temperature fluctuations are reduced. The soil is protected from erosion. Woodland sustains itself and is highly productive due to its diversity, and this leads to a gradual build up of fertility. The high humus content of the soil acts like a sponge to absorb water gradually and allows for the replenishment of ground water reservoirs. All the different available habitats allow a wide range of creatures to live in woodland, and the plants, insects and animals all work to create an altogether much more balanced and harmonious ecosystem compared to conventional agriculture.

It is possible to grow a variety of useful plants in an arrangement that emulates woodland - for example fruit and nut trees under- planted with smaller trees and shrubs, herbaceous, ground cover and climbing plants. This optimises use of the available area, and it is possible to produce edible fruits, nuts, seeds, leaves and roots throughout the year.

Edible Plants **3**

Unlike the majority of cultivated food plants the plants in this book have not been selectively bred to increase size of yield, reduce bitterness or increase sweetness, yet many of them are delicious and highly nutritious.

A woodland design may also include larger trees to provide natural shelter and wildlife habitats. Trees are the lungs of the planet; in effect they purify the air and have the potential to reduce the greenhouse effect by locking up carbon. Trees protect the soil from erosion, their fallen leaves improve soil structure, they can encourage rainfall, and regulate the flow of run off and ground water, helping to preventing flooding.

PFAF aims to recover lost or forgotten knowledge, in particular to encourage users of the database to learn more about the hundreds of medicinal plants that we can grow, and which may enable us to find safe natural alternatives to pharmaceutical drugs used today. And, of course, plants can also provide us with fibres for clothes, rope and paper, oils for lubricants, fuels, water proofing and wood preservatives, dyes, construction materials, and more.

The original PFAF project was inspired and informed by the principles and practice of Permaculture, which incorporates design methodologies and techniques to create genuinely sustainable, alternative land use systems, such as those outlined above. Readers unfamiliar with Permaculture are encouraged to find out more - the Permaculture Association Britain website at www.permaculture.org.uk being a good place to start.

General Disclaimer

To the best of our knowledge all the information contained herein is accurate. But of course we cannot guarantee that everyone will react positively to all plants described as edible in this book or to other plant uses suggested herein.

It is commonly known that many people suffer allergic reactions to conventional foods and products. Even amongst the more commonly eaten fruits, for example, there are plenty of instances where people react badly to them:

- Many people are allergic to strawberries and will come out in a rash if they eat them.

- Some people develop a rash if they touch the stems of parsnips.

- Potatoes become poisonous if they turn green.

- Eating large quantities of cabbage can adversely affect the thyroid gland.

We strongly recommend the following preventative precautions when trying anything new:

- Make sure you have identified the plant correctly

- Try a small quantity of anything you have not eaten before. Only increase the quantity consumed once you are satisfied that there are no undesirable side effects.

- When trying new soaps or skin applications try them on a very small area before proceeding to larger areas of the body. Look for any uncomfortable reactions or changes before widening the application.

No liability exists against Plants for a Future or any trustee, employee or contractor of Plants for a Future, nor can they be held responsible for any allergy, illness or injurious effect that any person or animal may suffer as a result of the use of information in this book or through using any of the plants mentioned in it.

Copyright 2013 by Plants For A Future
Second Edition
Plants For A Future is a charitable company limited by guarantee, registered in England and Wales.
Charity No. 1057719, Company No. 3204567
The PFAF website and Plants Database are at pfaf.org
Book Design: PembertonCreative.com

Alternative Food Crops

There are quite literally thousands of species of edible plants that can be grown in temperate climates, yet most people are only aware of the thirty or so species to be found in the Greengrocers, and many of these will have been imported. In this section we will give you a small selection of little known edible plants that are all fairly easily grown in most soils and often require less attention than many of our better known food crops. All are perennial unless stated otherwise.

Root Crops

Yam (Dioscorea batatas) -Few people realise that Yams can be grown outdoors in temperate climates like Britain. This is a perfectly hardy perennial species from China and its root is delicious baked. The only drawback is that it can be 3 foot long in good soils with the thickest part of the root at the bottom - quite a task to harvest, which is probably why it is not commercially cultivated. Propagation is either by replanting the top portion of the root, stem cuttings in late spring or by tubercles - baby tubers that are freely formed in the leaf axil of older plants and treated like seed, being sown in pots in the greenhouse, preferably as soon as ripe.

Oca (Oxalis tuberosa) -Comes from S. America. At least as hardy as the potato and grown in a similar way except it doesn t need to be earthed up and does not suffer all the diseases that potatoes do. The tubers do not form till late summer to autumn so yields can be low if you get early hard frosts, unless you protect the plants. When freshly harvested the tubers have a pleasant acid-lemon flavour and can be eaten raw or cooked. By storing them in the light the tubers become sweet, and some varieties in S. America, become so sweet that they are eaten as a fruit.

Earth Pea (Lathyrus tuberosus) - Is a rare native or naturalised plant in Britain. Not very high yielding, unfortunately, but the starch rich tubers are quite delicious baked. Plant in spring.

Tiger Nuts (Cyperus esculentus) -Not a nut at all, but another tuber. This plant is a weed in the tropics and subtropics but has proved to be hardy in temperate zones also. It is cultivated in Spain and is occasionally found for sale in Britain. It grows best in a moist soil, the tubers are about the size of peanuts and are abundantly produced. Eaten raw they make a very nice convenient snack when travelling. These tubers are quite unusual in being rich in oil. This oil is occasionally extracted for culinary and industrial use. Plant tubers in spring and harvest in late autumn. Mice love these tubers, so look out for any sign of burrowing.

Leaves

Mallow (Malva verticillata Crispa) -One of the very few annuals to get onto the list, this mallow is sometimes cultivated in the Mediterranean. The leaves have a mild flavour suitable for use in quantity in the salad bowl and can be harvested over many weeks. Sow in situ from April to June.

Campanula (Campanula versicolor) -This Mediterranean plant would grace any ornamental garden with its lovely blue harebell flowers. An evergreen perennial, its mild, slightly sweet flavoured leaves can be added in quantity to the salad bowl all year round. Sow seeds March/April in pots and plant out when large enough or divide in spring. It may not be hardy in some colder temperate regions.

Iron Cross Plant (Oxalis deppei) -Another one for the flower garden, this S. American bulbous plant has a pleasantly edible leaf, and its flowers are perhaps even nicer. They have a lemony flavour ideal for adding in small quantities to salads but should not be eaten in large quantities since they contain oxalic acid. Plant the bulbs in spring and they will provide fresh leaves and flowers throughout the summer. Harvest the bulbs when cut down by sharp frosts, when each bulb should have produced a cluster of bulbs on top of a white tap root. This tap root can be eaten raw or cooked - it has the texture of a crisp apple; but very little flavour.

Anise Hyssop (Agastache foeniculum) -A North American member of the mint family, the leaves have a rich aniseed flavour, delicious in salads. It usually comes out tops in tasting trials. Sow spring in pots and plant out when large enough.

Fruits

Elaeagnus Species -A genus of deciduous and evergreen shrubs mainly from Asia. A number of species have great potential as fruit crops. They are easily grown in most soils (but dislike very wet soils), tolerate very exposed situations and drought, are virtually untroubled by pests or diseases and produce nitrogen nodules on their roots thus helping to increase soil fertility. Some of the evergreen species (notably

E. pungens - E. x. ebbingei) ripen their fruits in late spring before any of our home-grown fruits are ripe and so are especially valuable. Other species will worth trying are the deciduous E. angustifolia and E. multifllora.

Japanese Raisin Tree (Hovenia dulcis) -A deciduous tree; as its name suggests, its fruits are said to taste like raisins.

Crataegus schraderana (Crataegus tournefortii) -A Hawthorn from the Mediterranean The ripe fruit is quite delicious, soft, sweet and almost literally melting in the mouth.

Edible Plants **5**

Tomatillo (Physalis ixocarpa /Physalis philadelphica) -Is a N. American annual grown in the same way as tomatoes (but does not need training) and used in all the ways you would cook tomatoes. It adds a lovely flavour to stews, is simple to grow, yields well and appears resistant to pests and diseases.

Seeds

Lupinus mutabilis -A South American annual Lupin with edible seeds. The seed has a similar nutritional value to the soya bean but is a lot easier to grow and is higher yielding in temperate climates. The original variety has bitter seeds, which can be removed by soaking overnight. New varieties are being developed with sweet seeds. Seed is sown late spring in situ.

Quinoa (Chenopodium quinoa) -Another easily grown S. American annual with edible seeds. The seeds look a bit like millet and can be used in all the ways rice is used in sweet or savoury dishes. The seed is coated with a bitter substance (saponins) which prevents it being eaten by birds. These saponins can be easily removed by soaking the seed overnight and then rinsing thoroughly. The young leaves make a tasty spinach. Sow late spring in situ - be careful not to weed the seedlings out since they look very much like Fat Hen, which can also be eaten like spinach.

Monkey Puzzle (Araucaria araucana) -An evergreen tree from Chile. If you have enough land and can afford to wait 30-40 years or would like to leave something of value for future generations, do seriously consider planting a grove of these trees. Female specimens produce a delicious almond-sized fatty seed which is a staple food in the tree s natural habitat. Trees do much better in the western part of Britain and can withstand severe exposure. The nuts are produced in cones about the size of a person s head, each cone contains up to 200 seeds and the mature cone falls to the ground before releasing the seeds, so harvesting is quite simple.

Maidenhair Tree (Ginkgo biloba) -A deciduous tree from China. When male and female trees are grown together, the female produces yellow plum-like fruits in autumn. When these fall to the ground and are squashed they give off a truly disgusting odour, but contained within the fruit is a seed which is considered a delicacy in China where it is usually roasted before being eaten. Another very easily grown tree.

Earth Pea (Lathyrus tuberosus)

Tiger Nuts (Cyperus esculentus)

Campanula (Campanula versicolor)

Mallow (Malva verticillata Crispa)

Yam (Dioscorea batatas)

Monkey Puzzle (Araucaria araucana)

Elaeagnus Species

Anise Hyssop (Agastache foeniculum)

Iron Cross Plant (Oxalis deppei)

Edible Plants 7

Quinoa (Chenopodium quinoa)

Maidenhair Tree (Ginkgo biloba)

Japanese Raisin Tree (Hovenia dulcis)

Crataegus schraderana

Oca (Oxalis tuberosa)

Tomatillo (Physalis ixocarpa)

Lupinus mutabilis

8   Plants For A Future: *www.pfaf.org*

Alternative Fruits

In a temperate zone like the UK you can grow a wealth of tasty fruits. However, all too often we limit ourselves to just a few well-known kinds, not realizing the vast wealth of other flavours we are missing. This section will look at some of these largely ignored fruits, with the hope of encouraging you to find space in your garden, allotment or whatever, where you will be able to grow and experience some of these flavours.

Although we are only going to look at the uncommon fruits that can be grown here, we would also strongly recommend that you grow a range of the more traditional crops. In fact you would be well advised to make sure that have planted at least some of the well known fruits before you even begin to consider some of the more unusual ones in this section.

So what are the fruits that we will not be looking at? Tree crops such as apples, pears, cherries and plums are discussed in all the many good books on fruit growing, as are the soft fruits such as raspberries, blackberries, red, white and blackcurrants, gooseberries, blueberries and strawberries. There are also several other fruits that are on the edge of their climatic tolerance here, but are none the less dealt with in most good books. These include grapes, figs, peaches and nectarines.

Having eliminated just about all the temperate zone fruits that most people are aware of, what is there left to talk about? A great deal, as I think you will agree after reading this section. All of the fruits we will be looking at here are, in general, of easy cultivation. Unless it says otherwise, they will be hardy in virtually all temperate zones, will succeed in most soils of reasonable fertility and will fruit best when grown in a sunny position, though will also do tolerably well in semi-shade. Almost all of them are trees or shrubs and so, with careful planning, it will be possible to grow various other crops with them in order to get better yields from the land and also to conserve and even improve fertility.

Most of the plants mentioned in this section will not have been selectively bred for heavier yields, or for flavour. None the less I think you will find that on the whole they will yield well, if not excellently, and, although individual tastes differ, it's likely that you will find at least some of the fruits mentioned here to be absolutely delicious. Another benefit of most of the plants mentioned here is that they are in general very hardy creatures and are less susceptible to pests and diseases. One of the problems in the past of selective breeding has been that, as we have selected for flavour and yield, so we have also unwittingly selected for plants that are less resistant to pests and diseases, and are also less tolerant of climatic extremes. Many of the plants mentioned below are much tougher creatures and will survive and fruit bountifully with very little attention from the grower.

Actinidia species

All members of this genus of climbing plants produce edible fruits, though they do not all do well in temperate zones. The best known species is A. deliciosa, the Kiwi Fruit. This is widely sold in greengrocers, though not many people realize it can be grown here successfully, at least in the warmer parts of the country. If you want fruit that you can pick then you will need to prune the plants to keep them small - if left unpruned they will romp away and can grow to the top of trees 20 metres or more tall! There are two main difficulties with this crop. The first is that, although the dormant plants are quite cold-hardy, the young shoots in spring are very susceptible to frost damage. It is therefore best to grow them on a westerly aspect so that they are protected from the morning sun but still get plenty of warm sunshine. The second problem is that plants are usually either male or female, so you need to grow at least one male plant for every 4 - 5 females in order to get fruit. There are some cultivars that do not need a male for fertilization, though these are said to have inferior fruits. When grown from seed, the vast majority of seedlings are male, so it is best to buy named varieties. Heywood is the female form that is most commonly offered, though others can sometimes be found. Tomuri is said to be a good pollinator.

Of the other species, probably the best to try in this country is A. arguta, the Tara Vine. This is even hardier than the Kiwi, its fruit is rather smaller but this is not covered with hairs and so can be eaten without peeling.

Amelanchier species

Although called Juneberries, the fruit actually ripens around the middle of July. This fruit is a bit smaller than blackcurrants, is sweet and juicy and has a definite flavour of apples. The main problem with this plant is that it is also a favourite fruit of the birds and so there is a bit of a race as to who gets there first. If you want to eat the fully ripe fruit then you will probably have to use some netting or other protective device. There are many species to choose from, our favourites include:-

Amelanchier alnifolia. This is a shrub that rarely grows more than 2 - 3 metres tall in this country and so is relatively easy to protect from the birds, and produces very sweet and juicy Juneberries. Once established, this plant will often produce suckers and can in time form thickets.

Amelanchier alnifolia semiintegrifolia is a very similar plant to the above, but with smaller fruits that ripen a week or two later.

Amelanchier laevis is a somewhat taller species that can reach 9 metres in height.

Edible Plants

Amelanchier stolonifera. This is a relatively low-growing shrub, often no more than 2 metres tall. It can sucker quite freely, though only forms a slowly expanding clump. A very tasty fruit, vying with A. alnifolia as the favourite in this genus.

Arbutus unedo

The Strawberry Tree is a delightful evergreen for the garden. The species can grow up to 9 metres tall, though there are cultivars that rarely go above 2 metres. The plant produces beautiful lily-of-the-valley type flowers in late autumn and is particularly eye-catching at this time since it is also ripening the fruit from the previous year's flowering. These fruits do look rather like a strawberry, especially from a distance, but unfortunately do not taste like strawberries. Indeed, many people find them quite bland and the latin name unedo means I eat one [only] suggesting that they are not a worthwhile food. However, some people find them sweet and tasty, though they do have a rather gritty texture. But when you are getting a succulent fruit in winter you can forgive it a little grittiness. This plant does not do well in the colder parts of the country. It is surprisingly wind-tolerant, however, and grows well near the coast. If you want a dwarf variety, then look out for Compacta, Elfin King or Rubra.

Berberis species

All members of this genus have edible fruits, though they tend to be rather acid in flavour and have rather too many seeds. Our native B. vulgaris used to be cultivated for its fruit, which ripens in late summer. There was a seedless cultivar, though it may not still be in cultivation. A deciduous shrub, it grows well in hedgerows, though it is considered a pest in cereal-growing areas because it is an alternate host for a disease of cereals.

Of particular merit is B. darwinii. This evergreen shrub can grow to 3 or 4 metres tall and makes an excellent wind-resistant hedge, succeeding even in maritime areas. The fruit ripens in July-August and is adored by the birds. At first it is very acid, but if allowed to fully ripen it loses most of this acidity and has a lovely flavour.

Cornus species

There are some wonderful fruits in this genus. C. masi, the Cornelian Cherry is a deciduous shrub that can reach 5 metres or more in height. It produces yellow flowers in midwinter and is particularly attractive at this time. The fruit ripens in late summer and needs to be fully ripe or it is very astringent. There is quite a degree of variability in size and quality of fruit. There used to be special cultivated varieties, but these may no longer exist. The fruits can get as large as 2cm long and 1.5cm wide. This species can also be grown as a hedge and is quite wind tolerant.

C. kousa, the Japanese Dogwood, is a deciduous tree that can grow up to 10 metres tall. It ripens its fruit in late summer, these are the size of very large strawberries and have a succulent flesh with an exquisite flavour. The skin is fairly soft and can be eaten with the fruit, but it does have a decidedly bitter flavour. Perhaps the best approach is to bite a small hole in the skin and then suck out the flesh. It is really like a luscious tropical fruit. The form most often found in gardens is C. kousa chinensis, this is said to grow and fruit better than the species, though maybe there isn t much difference.

Crataegus species

Hawthorns are one of the very best fruiting genera for temperate areas. There are many species with delicious fruits, the following are particularly recommended. In general the fruit is about the size of cherries and ripens in late summer:-

Crataegus arnoldiana. A tree that grows to 7 metres tall, the fruit is juicy and sweet.

Crataegus baroussana. A shrub to about 2 metres, the fruit is not quite as nice as the species above. This plant is probably only hardy in warmer temperate zones.

Crataegus douglasii. Growing up to 9 metres tall, the fruit is similar to C. arnoldiana.

Crataegus ellwangeriana. Up to 6 metres tall, with very similar fruit to C. arnoldiana.

Crataegus festiva. Growing 3 - 4 metres tall, the fruit is one of the best in the genus.

Crataegus pensylvanica. A tall shrub to 9 metres tall, it always seems to produce heavy crops of very tasty fruits.

Crataegus schraderiana. A tree to 6 metres tall. When the fruit is fully ripe it almost literally melts in the mouth.

Crataegus tanacetifolia. Growing up to 10 metres tall, the fruit is yellow in colour and rather like a very rich apple in flavour.

Diospyros species

A genus of deciduous trees, the true Persimmon, D. kaki, is not a reliable fruiter in temperate climates, which is a shame since it is one of the most exquisite fruits it is possible to eat. However, the following species produce similar tasting, if much smaller, fruits:-

Diospyros lotus. The DATE PLUM grows up to 9 metres tall.

10   Plants For A Future: www.pfaf.org

The fruit does not often ripen on the tree, but if you either leave it on the ground when it falls in autumn, or harvest it and store it in a cool place such as a garage, it will continue to ripen. Don't eat it until it is squidgy-soft or it will be harsh and astringent.

Diospyros virginiana. The American Persimmon can make a massive tree in its native range, though it seldom grows larger than 10 metres in this country. The fruit can be 2cm or more in diameter and is harvested and used in the same way as D. lotus.

Elaeagnus species

If you want to harvest a fresh fruit from your garden in spring, then this is the plant for you! The following species are especially recommended:-

Elaeagnus cordifolia. A shrub growing to about 4 metres tall and wide, it is probably not hardy in the colder areas of the country. This produces the largest and earliest fruits.

Elaeagnus macrophylla. Grows about 3 metres tall and wide. Not hardy in the colder areas of the country. Selected cultivars have very good-sized fruits.

Elaeagnus x ebbingei. A very common hedging plant, it can crop prolifically when given suitable conditions.

Fuchsia species

A genus of deciduous shrubs, though most of them are not very hardy and act more as herbaceous perennials in all but the mildest areas of the country. Fuchsia are commonly grown ornamentals, all of them produce edible fruits, though these often have a less than desirable aftertaste. Our favourite is F. splendens - but this is rather tender and will only succeed outdoors in the mildest areas of the country. It grows best in a shady position and does well even on a north-facing wall. It will succeed in full sun but can look rather burnt in such a position. The fruit is about the size and shape of a baby s finger, it is soft and juicy with a very pleasant slightly acid flavour. If you cannot grow this plant in your area then there are many other hardier forms available. The best thing to do is to try some fruits from plants that you or your friends might already be growing. If you cannot find any you like, try getting hold of the cultivars Tresco or Globosa.

Gaultheria shallon

An evergreen shrub to about 1.2 metres tall, it grows well in dappled woodland shade. The Shallon requires an acid soil, producing its fruit in the latter half of summer. This is about the size of a blackcurrant, it is pleasantly juicy though does not have a strong flavour. If you want a strong flavour then its diminutive relate, G. procumbens might be for you. Another plant for an acid soil and the dappled shade of woodland, it grows only 15cm tall and makes a good ground cover. The fruit ripens over a long period, fruits can be eaten from late summer round to late winter. These fruits are about the size of a large blackcurrant and have a very distinctive flavour that strongly resembles the Germolene of hospital waiting rooms! Surprisingly there are a number of people who really like this fruit, but perhaps it is acceptable only in small doses; it certainly leaves the mouth feeling clean and fresh.

Hippophae salicifolia

The Willow-Leaved Sea Buckthorn is a vigorous large deciduous shrub that suckers freely and so is not suitable for places where space is at a premium. A light-demanding species, it will not fruit well in the shade. A bacteria that lives on the roots fixes atmospheric nitrogen, so this is a plant that helps to fertilize the soil and to feed neighbouring plants. The fruit is only about 5mm in diameter and has a sharp lemon flavour. It cannot be eaten raw in any quantity, but makes an excellent juice, syrup or jam. Research has shown that this plant produces the most nutritious fruit yet discovered in temperate zones, regular use may prevent cancer, and large quantities have been shown to reverse the growth of cancer tumours. The fruit ripens in early autumn and hangs well on the plant - it can still be picked in late winter.

Morus nigra

The Black Mulberry is fairly well known, but is all too rarely grown for its fruit. A deciduous tree, it can reach 10 metres in height but is usually smaller. The fruit ripens in late summer, it looks rather like a large raspberry, is very juicy and has a refreshing acid flavour.

Myrtus ugni (Ugni molinae)

You are going to have to live in a very mild area of the country to enjoy this fruit, but it is one of Ken Fern s favourites. An evergreen shrub, it grows about 2 metres tall and wide and is reasonably wind-resistant. The fruit, which is a bit smaller than a blackcurrant, has a delicious aromatic flavour that has been described as a cross between a wild strawberry and a guava. Ken said No words can do justice to this fruit - you have to eat it to believe it. To us it is just ambrosia.

Physalis peruviana

The Goldenberry is another plant for the milder areas of the country. An evergreen shrub in its native tropical environment, the leaves and shoots will be killed by the first

Edible Plants **11**

serious frosts of autumn. However, the plant can be grown as an annual in much the same way as tomatoes, and in the milder areas of the country the roots will often survive the winter and send out new shoots in late spring. Applying a good mulch in the autumn will help here. The fruit is produced in its own paper bag, just like the Chinese lanterns to which it is related. When the fruit is fully ripe, these bags tun brown and dry. The fruit is golden yellow in colour, it is about 25mm in diameter, though it can vary considerably. It is somewhat tomato-like in flavour and appearance, though the taste is much richer with a hint of tropical luxuriance. The fruit starts to ripen in mid to late summer, late-ripening fruits can be stored in their bags for up to three months.

Rosa rugosa

The Ramanas Rose is a fairly common hedge plant in temperate regions. A fast-growing and vigorously suckering deciduous shrub, it grows up to 2 metres tall. It is very tolerant of maritime exposure and of poor sandy soils. The fruit ripens from mid to late summer, it is deliciously sweet and has a very rich flavour. A rather fiddly fruit to eat, however, because there is only a fairly thin layer of fruit over a centre comprised of many seeds. It is important not to eat these seeds since they have small hairs on them and these can act as gastric irritants.

Rubus species

There are many members of this genus that are used for food. You probably already know blackberries, raspberries, loganberries and some of the many hybrid berries such as sunberries. There are a couple of less well-known species:

R. nepalensis, the Nepalese Raspberry, is a very low-growing evergreen shrub that makes an excellent ground cover. The plants seldom get taller than 20cm, but instead send out fairly vigorous ground-hugging stems that root at intervals as they scramble across the ground. Although the books say that the plant is only hardy in the milder areas, it is growing and fruiting at Cambridge Botanic gardens, which gets quite cold winters. The fruit is produced in mid to late summer. It is about two thirds the size of conventional raspberries and has a very nice acid flavour.

Another member of this genus worthy of attention is R. phoenicolasius, the Japanese Wineberry. A deciduous shrub, it can grow up to 3 metres tall. It has biennial stems in the same way as other raspberries, new stems being produced each year that flower in their second year and then die. The orange fruit is about 10mm in diameter and is produced in late summer. It is very juicy and has a very nice raspberry flavour. One very useful aspect of this fruit is that the plant very conveniently wraps up each developing fruit in the calyx of the flower, only unwrapping it as the fruit ripens.

This does mean that the fruit is almost always maggot-free.

Taxus baccata

The Yew is a very slow-growing evergreen tree, it can eventually reach 15 metres in height though there are many smaller cultivars available. It is a very tolerant plant, growing in acid or alkaline conditions, in sun or shade (fruiting well even in fairly dense shade) and in windy positions. All parts of the plant are very toxic, except the sweet and juicy fruit. This ripens from late summer through the autumn. Most people who are willing to try this fruit find it delicious, though some are put off by its texture that is rather mucilaginous (or snotty to put it more bluntly). Be careful not to bite into the seed when eating this fruit - it is best to spit this out though it will do no harm if you swallow it whole. If you should accidentally bite into the seed (and you will immediately know by the bitter flavour in your mouth), then you should straight away spit it out to avoid any possibility of poisoning.

We do hope this section encourages you to try growing at least some of them. For more details on the nutritional properties of fruits see the section: Fruit - Food of the Gods.

Edible Plants 13

Alternative Root Crops

Although this section is titled Alternative Root Crops, it is not restricted to the botanist's definition of a root, but also discusses all types of underground storage organs including tubers, bulbs and corms.

The traditional root crops grown in temperate regions are potatoes, parsnips, carrots, beetroot, onions, turnips and swede with lesser-known plants such as Jerusalem artichokes, celeriac, Chinese artichokes, radishes and winter radishes (mooli) playing a minor role. Of these, potatoes are by far the most important. They are very high yielding and, because they have a mild flavour that goes well with many other foods, they are widely used as a staple crop. They do have many disadvantages though, especially in their high susceptibility to disease and in particular to blight, for which there is no acceptable organic treatment as yet.

Most of these traditional crops have been selectively bred, sometimes over thousands of years, for improved flavour and yields. Potatoes, for example, were extremely low yielding when first introduced from South America. The wild carrot has a thin woody root that bears little comparison to the cultivated plant. This selective breeding, however, has not been an unconditional success. Potatoes must be one of our most disease-prone crops - sometimes it seems you only have to look at them and they go down with blight. Carrots suffer from root fly and violet root rot, assuming you can get them past the seedling stage without them being eaten by slugs or overtaken by weeds.

Many of the plants mentioned in this section, on the other hand, have never been bred as a food crop so yields will often be rather lower. They are, however, usually much less prone to pests and diseases and so are often easier to grow. They are also in general much more robust plants and can often be grown in a semi-wild setting and just harvested as required. There is an added bonus to this, since with many of the plants, such as the Erythronium species, it is possible to grow them amongst other plants and so their yield is an extra bonus from the land.

The plants detailed in the list below are rather a diverse bunch and as a result they have a variety of cultivation needs. Unless the text says otherwise you can assume that the plant will succeed in full sun or light shade in most well- drained soils, and will yield much better if the soil is fairly rich in organic matter.

Apios americana

The GROUND NUT is an herbaceous climbing plant, reaching about 4ft tall. It belongs to the pea and bean family and, like many other members of that family, it helps to enrich the soil with nitrogen by means of bacteria that live on the roots and fix atmospheric nitrogen. The root, which is unusually high in protein, has a very pleasant sweet taste when baked. It can be cooked in many other ways and can also be eaten raw, though it is rather tough to chew. *(One correspondent on the PFAF site says that this plant has some a nti nutritional factors, such as trypsin inhibitors ... so it should be cooked before being eaten)*

Yields from the wild plant are fairly low, though they are much better if the plant is left in the ground for 2 years before harvesting. There are a number of cultivated forms being developed, however, that have much higher yields and the plant has been recommended for commercial cultivation. This species can be grown along the sunny edges of a woodland garden and either allowed to twine its way into small shrubs or given some supports to climb into.

Camassia quamash

QUAMASH is a beautiful bulbous plant that grows about 2ft tall and flowers in early summer. It belongs to the onion family (though it does not taste like it) and the flowers look a little bit like a bluebell. Plants can succeed in short grass, so long as this is not too vigorous, and can therefore be grown in the light shade of a tree in the lawn. Do not cut the grass during the time when the bulbs come into growth until they die down in mid summer. Quamash bulbs are about the size of a small onion; they are rich in starch and develop a very nice sweet flavour when slowly baked. They can also be eaten raw but their texture is somewhat gummy .

Quamash was a staple food of the N. American Indians. Local tribes would move to the quamash fields in the early autumn and, whilst some people harvested the bulbs, others would dig a pit, line it with boulders then fill it with wood and set fire to it. The fire would heat the boulders and the harvested bulbs would then be placed in the pit and the whole thing covered with earth and the bulbs left to cook slowly for 2 days. The pit would then be opened and the Indians would feast on the bulbs until they could eat no more. Whatever was left would be dried and stored for winter use. It is possible to grow quamash in an orchard - the plants will die down before the first apples are harvested and so will not get in the way. The bulbs should increase of their own accord and then can be harvested in much the same way as the Indians, though you might not choose to eat them in quite the same way!

Cyperus esculentus

TIGER NUTS are a noxious weed in the tropics, but are also a cultivated crop and can sometimes be found on sale in temperate regions. Plants grow about 2ft tall and prefer a sunny position in a soil that is on the wet side.

Edible Plants **15**

Tiger nuts grown by Ken Fern in Cornwall seemed to be quite hardy (forms of the plant have become naturalised as far north as Alaska) but yields were disappointing. This was at least partly because of problems getting the tubers to come into new growth in the spring. They are normally harvested after the first frosts have cut back top growth and then stored in moist sand in a cool frost-free place. In early spring they can be potted and put into a polytunnel, but they can take months before coming into growth and consequently do not manage to get in a full growing season in Britain. (Perhaps this will change with global warming.) The tubers are small and rather fiddly but they have a delicious sweet flavour. They can be eaten raw but are very chewy unless soaked beforehand. Tiger nuts are unusual amongst roots in that they contain a relatively high level of oil and this is sometimes extracted and used as a high-grade food oil.

Dioscorea batatas

This hardy YAM is cultivated in Japan as a root crop but, although it grows very well in temperate regions, it has never been grown much in Britain. A climbing plant reaching 8ft or more in height, it requires a sunny position in a fertile well-drained soil and should be given some support on which to twine. If you have a deep rich soil then the root can be up to 3ft long and weigh 4lbs or more. Rich in starch, it is best baked but can also be boiled, added to stews etc. There is no strong flavour, but the overall taste is very acceptable and it can be eaten in quantity as a staple crop. It is similar to a floury potato. You can propagate the plant by cutting off the top few inches of root and replanting this. An easier method is to harvest the small tubercles (baby tubers that look a little like small bulbs) that are formed in the leaf axils along the stems. Collect them in late summer, once they are easily detached from the plant, and pot them up immediately in a cold greenhouse. They will remain dormant in the winter and then come into growth in the spring. Plant them out in the summer when they are in active growth.

Erythronium species

DOG'S TOOTH VIOLETS are dainty woodland bulbs. They row about 1ft tall and flower in early spring, disappearing completely by early summer. Grow them in light shade, and also consider growing them under trees in the orchard or on a lawn. Suitable varieties increase very freely when well sited and the bulb, which can be 3 inches long and about an inch wide, has a pleasant sweet taste. It can be eaten raw or cooked. Any of the species can be used, though these are quite expensive to obtain and many people would consider the plant too beautiful to eat. The cultivars White Beauty and Pagoda are easily grown forms that are relatively cheap to buy and usually divide freely in the garden.

Helianthus tuberosus

JERUSALEM ARTICHOKE is a fairly well known root crop that is sometimes seen in greengrocers. The plants are very vigorous, growing up to 10ft tall, and some people have been growing them successfully as part of a woodland garden, planting them on the sunnier side of the woodland. Slugs absolutely adore the young shoots in spring, so give the plants some protection at this time of the year - a mulch of oak leafmould works well. The main drawback of this root is that over half of the carbohydrate it contains is in the form of inulin and the body cannot absorb this. It does mean that you can eat quite a lot of it without putting on weight, but it does also mean that many people will find the inulin fermenting in their gut causes quite a bit of wind! The tubers can be eaten raw or cooked and the flavour improves if they are left in the ground until frosted.

Lathyrus tuberosus

The TUBEROUS PEA has one of the most pleasant tubers to eat. Unfortunately the plant is rather low yielding and so unless improved cultivars are developed it will never become more than an occasional delicacy. Grow the plant on the sunny side of woodland, or perhaps in a cultivated bed amongst shrubs. It grows about 3ft tall and twines around available supports. It is quite a weak climber, however, and is more likely to sprawl across the ground. A member of the pea and bean family, the plant will enrich the soil with nitrogen.

Lilium lancifolium

The TIGER LILY is often grown in the flower garden but in the Orient it is cultivated for its edible bulb. In fact when grown as a root crop the Chinese actually pick off the flower buds to stimulate the production of larger bulbs. All other members of this genus also produce edible bulbs, though these can often have a bitter flavour. When baked, lily bulbs taste rather like potatoes. One word of warning with this particular species - although tolerant of virus disease, it can often act as a carrier of these diseases and so becomes a vector infecting other species. It is therefore wise to either grow this species well away from your other lilies, or to avoid growing the other species if you grow this one. The plant is easily propagated by means of bulbils that form in the leaf axils. Simply pot these up in the summer when they part easily from the plant and then plant them out in the spring 18 months later. Allow some of the bulbils to fall to the ground to see if the plant will maintain itself without your help.

Lomatium cous (Cogswellia cous)

Lomatium cous comes from western N. America and grows on dry often open rocky slopes and flats. It is often found with sagebrush, is most common in foothills and lowland areas but is occasionally found above the tree line. The root is eaten cooked; it can also be dried and ground into a flour and can then be mixed with cereal flours or added to soups etc. When dug up in the spring, it is said to have a parsnip-like flavour. Other members of this genus, in particular L. geyeri and L. macrocarpum may also be of interest. Known as BISCUIT ROOTS, they have celery-flavoured roots that can be eaten raw or cooked. The N. American Indians dried and ground them into flour and then either mixed it with cereal flours or added it to soups etc. They also mixed the flour with water, flattened it into cakes then sun-dried or baked them for use on journeys, the taste is said to be somewhat like stale biscuits.

Orogenia linearifolia

INDIAN POTATO grows to about 15cm tall on open mountain sides and ridges, often in sandy or gravelly soils, and especially near vernal snowbanks where it blooms as soon as the snow melts. It is found in much of western N. America. The root is said to have a pleasant crisp taste, though the outer skin has a slightly bitter taste. Available at almost any time of the year, its only drawback is that it is a bit small and fiddly to harvest in quantity.

Oxalis tuberosa

OCA has had a long history of cultivation in S. America where it is one of the three most popular root crops. The tuber can be 3 inches long and about an inch wide - yields per plant are often not much below that from potatoes. The plants are about as hardy as potatoes, tolerating light frosts but dying down in harder frosts. In mild areas the tubers can be left in the ground and harvested as required (so long as the ground does not get too wet in the winter), but in colder areas it is best to harvest them when the plant dies down and store them in a cool frost-free place. The tubers have a lemon flavour when first harvested but if you leave them out in the sun for a week or so they become quite sweet. Some cultivars, in fact, become so sweet that they are eaten rather like a fruit in S. America. The main disadvantage of this plant is that it does not start to form tubers until around the autumn equinox and so, if there is an early heavy frost, yields will be very low.

Perideridia gairdneri

YAMPA root can be eaten raw or cooked and is said to have a pleasant sweet and nutty taste that can be eaten in quantity. The flavour is said to be somewhat like a superior parsnip and the dried root is said to be so nice that it is an almost irresistible nibble. The root is best harvested when the plant is dormant and can also be dried for later use or ground

into a flour and used in porridges, cakes etc. Yampa grows in woodland and wet meadows in its native range, which stretches from California along the west of N. America to Saskatchewan in Canada, and so it should be perfectly hardy in Britain

Polymnia edulis (Smallanthus sonchifolius)

YACON is often cultivated for its edible root in S. America, where yields of 15 tons per acre have been achieved. This frost-tender plant grows about 3ft tall and can be cultivated like potatoes. It requires a 6 -7 month growing season so would probably not succeed in the colder parts of temperate regions. It is best started off in pots even in the warmer areas. A fast-growing and tolerant plant, it succeeds in poor soils though it yields better in soils of at least reasonable quality and requires a sunny position. The large root is crisp and juicy and in some cultivars is also incredibly sweet, though the skin is often bitter. In S. America it is eaten more like a fruit than a root. The nutritional value is low, however, because much of the carbohydrate in the root is in the form of inulin. The human gut is unable to assimilate inulin and so it passes straight through the digestive system. This makes it an ideal food if you are on a diet to lose weight and want to eat enough to fill yourself up! A gentle warning, however, inulin causes fermentation in the gut of some people, leading to unpleasant wind. Inulin can be easily converted to fructose, a sugar that is safe for diabetics to use, and so it is sometimes used to make a sweetener.

Psoralea esculenta

BREADROOT is a well known N. American Indian food. Perfectly hardy in this country, it requires a sunny position and like many members of the pea and bean family it helps to enrich the soil with nitrogen. The root can be eaten raw, cooked or be dried for later use. The dried root can also be ground into a flour and used in cakes, porridges etc. Starchy and glutinous, the raw root is said to have a sweetish turnip-like taste. The plant has in the past been recommended for commercial cultivation and has the potential to be high yielding.

Sagittaria species

Most if not all members of this genus produce edible tubers and a number aare cultivated for this, especially in the Orient. They succeed in wet soils but are best in water 1 - 2ft deep. S. sagittifolia, the ARROWHEAD, is a native species and this is the plant that is most frequently cultivated. Its tubers can often be purchased in Chinese shops in this country and this is one of the best ways of obtaining plants, though the tubers need to be fresh if they are to grow away before rotting. The tubers are starchy with a distinct flavour that some people

Edible Plants

have likened to potatoes. There is a slight bitterness, but this is mainly in the skin that is best removed after cooking. They make a very acceptable stodgy part of the meal. The tubers can also be dried and ground into flour, this flour can then be used as a gruel etc. or can be added to cereal flours and used in making bread, biscuits or cakes. The tubers, which can be produced up to 1 metre from the plant, are best harvested in the late summer as the leaves die down. They should not be eaten raw. Other species to try include: - S. cuneata, the WAPATO, S. graminea; and S. latifolia, the DUCK POTATO.

Sium sisarum

SKIRRET grows about 4ft tall and used to be cultivated for its edible root. This can be eaten raw or cooked and is firm, sweet and floury but with a woody core. The plant is very pest and disease-resistant. It requires plenty of moisture in the growing season otherwise its root will tend to be very fibrous. Make sure that you do not grow the sub-species S. sisarum lancifolium since this is very unlikely to produce good quality roots.

Stachys affinis

CHINESE ARTICHOKES grow about 1ft tall and dislike dry soils or shade. Their roots are rather small and fiddly, though overall yields are quite good and they have a pleasant flavour with a nice crisp juicy texture. They can be cooked or eaten raw, perhaps chopped up and added to a mixed salad.

(Incidentally, there is an easy way of cleaning small and fiddly roots. You half fill a bucket with water, add a good quantity of dirt so that you have a nice muddy mixture. You then add all the roots that you want to wash and stir the mixture for a few minutes. Then tip out the roots and rinse them - they will be lovely and clean, ready for use.)

Tropaeolum tuberosum

This beautiful climbing plant is only hardy in the milder areas of temperate regions, where it can reach a height of 6 ft or more. It flowers freely in late summer and then dies down with the first hard frosts in the autumn. It produces a number of edible tubers near the soil surface and can be quite heavy yielding. In mild winter areas the tubers can be left in the ground (though it would be a good idea to mulch them), in colder areas they should be harvested and stored in much the same way as dahlias. The tubers are quite popular in S. America, but they are probably best described as an acquired taste. The rather peppery flavour is improved considerably if the tubers are cooked and then frozen before eating them. (You can warm them up again if you like!) Ken Fern found that if the tubers were left in the ground and then harvested after being frosted the flavour was better.

The tuber is considered by people in the Andes to lower the sex-drive and many men refuse to eat it, whilst recommending it for women! Clinical trials have indicated a reduction of up to 45% in some male hormones when the tuber forms a considerable part of the diet, but no loss in fertility has been observed. The growing plant is very resistant to diseases and insects; it contains nematocidal, bactericidal and insecticidal compounds. The main problem with growing this plant in temperate regions is that the tubers are not formed until the shorter days of autumn and if you get an early frost then yields can be very low. The cultivar Ken Aslett is probably the best form available in Britian; it comes into flower earlier and produces larger tubers than the species type.

Typha latifolia

The British native REEDMACE is potentially one of the most productive rootcrops that can be grown. Not only that, its native habitat is marshy ground and shallow water where it makes a superb wildlife habitat. Reedmace might therefore be a productive crop in areas prone to flooding which would otherwise be difficult and expensive to protect.

The root can be eaten raw or cooked. It can be boiled and eaten like potatoes or macerated and boiled to yield sweet syrup. The root can also be dried, ground into flour and then used as a thickener in soups etc or added to cereal flours. Rich in protein, this flour is used to make biscuits etc. Yields of 3 tonnes of flour per acre are possible, which compares very favourably with wheat. The plant also has many other edible and non-edible uses that we will not enumerate here. T. angustifolia is a closely related British native plant with the same uses.

Apios americana GROUND NUT

Camassia quamash QUAMASH

Helianthus tuberosus ARTICHOKE

Polymnia edulis YACON

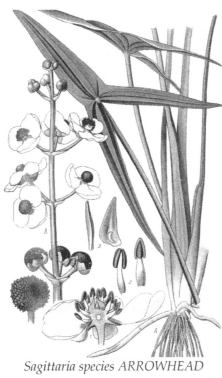
Sagittaria species ARROWHEAD

Sium sisarum SKIRRET

Perideridia gairdneri YAMPA

Orogenia linearifolia INDIAN POTATO

Lomatium cous (Cogswellia cous)

Edible Plants

Stachys affinis CHINESE ARTICHOKES

Tropaeolum tuberosum

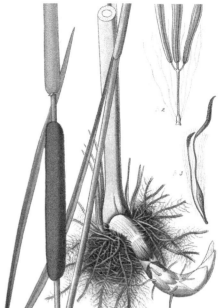
Typha latifolia REEDMACE

Lilium lancifolium TIGER LILY

Psoralea esculenta BREADROOT

Erythronium DOG S TOOTH VIOLETS

Alternative Edible Leaves

Most of the leaf crops we grow for food are annual plants - with all the work and problems associated with the growing of annuals such as digging the soil, preparing seed beds, sowing seed, weeding, more weeding and yet more weeding. This section is going to look at a few of the many perennial leaf crops that can be grown in the garden with a fraction of the work and often with higher total yields. Whilst many perennial food crops can be slow to begin yielding, growing perennial plants for their leaves will usually give you at least a small crop in the first year and this will then increase in the following years. The variety in tastes and textures is quite staggering - especially for those people who regard a salad as consisting of the standard lettuce, spring onions, radish, cucumber and tomatoes.

By growing some of the plants described here, it would be possible to have salads including many different types of leaves, some of which will have a mild flavour and can be used in quantity to form the bulk of the salad, others will have stronger tastes and will be used more as flavourings. These stronger flavours can be very sweet, often with a liquorice-like flavour. They can be rather acid, with a lemon-like flavour. Some of them have a more savoury taste, often with a garlic or mustard flavour, whilst others are pungently hot. Not only is there this wonderful range of flavours to choose from, but leaves are also the most nutritious of all the foods we eat. Amongst their many benefits to the health, they are rich sources of vitamins and minerals, contain a very good quality protein and supply essential dietary fibre. See the section Green Gold - The Leaves of Life for more details of this.

The range of plants listed below is quite diverse, and species suitable for any niche in the garden will be found. It is therefore very difficult to give general notes on their cultivation needs, though a very brief guide will be given. Fuller details on each plant can be found in the pfaf.org online database.

Agastache foeniculum

ANISE HYSSOP grows about 75cm tall and wide, preferring a sunny position and a dry well-drained soil. It is not hardy in the colder areas of temperate regions, tolerating winter temperatures down to between -5 and -10 c. Although easy to grow, the young growth in spring is very susceptible to slug damage and you might need to give the plant some protection at this time. The plant flowers in mid to late summer, although not very showy, these flowers are very attractive to bees and butterflies.

The leaves are available from mid spring until early autumn and have a sweet aniseed flavour. They make a delicious addition to the salad bowl, and can also be used to flavour cooked foods, especially acid fruits. The only drawback to the leaves is that they tend to have a drying effect in the mouth and so cannot be eaten in quantity.

Allium species

All members of this genus, which includes the onion, leek and garlic, are edible. By careful selection, it is possible to provide fresh leaves all year round for use in salads and as flavouring in cooked dishes. The flavours range from mild onion right through to the strongest garlic. We will only give a very brief list here of some of our more favourite species, for more information please see the pfaf.org website on Allium species - the Perennial Onions , which deals with this genus in much greater detail. Unless stated otherwise, all members of this genus require a well-drained soil and a sunny position. In general they do not grow well with weed competition, though there are exceptions.

Allium cepa. This species includes the common ONION, which will not be discussed here. There is, however, a very interesting and productive form called the EVERLASTING ONION. This grows in a similar manner to chives, quickly forming a large clump. The leaves have a mild onion flavour and can be used like spring onions in salads or as a flavouring in cooked foods. The plant is evergreen and very hardy, so it can provide its edible leaves all year round, even in quite severe winters.

Allium fistulosum. The WELSH ONION is rather similar to the above species in growth habit and flavour. It is not quite so winter hardy, though, and in severe winters will die back to the ground. However, it will soon grow away again with the return of warmer weather in the spring.

Allium neapolitanum. DAFFODIL GARLIC grows about 30cm tall, forming a gradually expanding clump. This leaf first produces has a delicious sweetness In the mouth, followed by a moderately strong garlic flavour. A plant for a warm sunny bed, it is not very winter hardy outside the south of Britain. It comes into growth in the autumn, provides its leaves all through the winter then flowers in the spring and dies down until the following autumn.

Allium schoenoprasum. CHIVES are perhaps too well known to be included here, but it is worth reminding you that they are a very productive crop and can supply their mild, onion flavoured leaves from late winter until late autumn.

Allium triquetrum. THREE-CORNERED LEEK has become naturalised in south-western Britain where it often forms large colonies in lightly shaded places. It is an ideal plant for growing at the base of a hedge or on a woodland edge. Like the previous species, this is a plant that grows in the winter

Edible Plants **21**

and is dormant in the summer. The leaves have an onion-garlic flavour and can be used in quantity in salads.

Like the previous species, this plant is not very cold tolerant though by giving it the protection of the trees and shrubs in the woodland it will succeed in many areas.

Allium tuberosum. GARLIC CHIVES forms a slowly spreading clump about 30cm tall. As the common name suggests, the leaves have a very pleasant flavour very much like a cross between garlic and chives. They are available from the middle of spring until late autumn. The plant is capable of growing all year round in warmer climates and so, if you pot them up in late summer and grow them on the kitchen windowsill, you will be able to pick the leaves all through the winter.

Allium ursinum. WILD GARLIC is a native plant and is often found forming large colonies in woodlands. If it is not growing wild near you, then it is quite easy to establish the plant in a shady part of the garden. It will be more than capable of looking after itself and will provide you with its garlic flavoured leaves from late winter until late spring

Atriplex halimus

The SALT BUSH is an evergreen shrub growing about 1.5 metres tall and wide. It requires a very sunny position in a well-drained soil and makes a good hedge. Instead of spending all your time trimming hedges, grow this plant and trim it by harvesting the young growth for use in salads and as a spinach substitute. The leaves have a distinctive salty taste. The only problem we have with it is that it produces very little growth in the winter and so harvesting at this time of the year has to be very moderate. The plant soon bursts into vigorous growth with the warmer spring weather and can then be harvested in quantity. When picking the leaves, do not strip them from the stems but instead pick the whole stem. Harvest just the top 3 - 5cm if using them in salads, but harvest young shoots up to 25cm long if cooking them. When lightly steamed, the leaves retain their flavour and texture well, making an excellent spinach substitute.

The plant is very wind resistant and is tolerant of very salty soils and also of dry conditions. It makes an excellent shelter hedge in maritime areas. It is not cold-hardy in all areas, being defoliated if temperatures drop much below -5 c for any period of time, and often being killed at temperatures much below -10 c.

Brassica oleracea

This species includes some of our most common vegetables such as the cabbage, cauliflower and Brussels sprouts. Whilst these plants are biennial, there are also a few perennial forms. Although not widely known, these perennials can be amongst the most productive food plants that can be grown in the garden. They all grow best in a sunny position and succeed in most soils, doing well in heavy clays. They do not like very acid conditions.

The true wild form of B. oleracea is the WILD CABBAGE, which can still be found growing by the sea in many parts of the country. A short-lived evergreen perennial, it can grow up to 1.2 metres tall. The leaves have a stronger flavour than the cultivated cabbages, and at times can have a distinct bitterness, especially in the winter. However, you may find this to be a very acceptable cooked vegetable. Plants will usually live for 3 - 5 years, though some can reach 10 years old or more.

Whilst most of the plants developed from the wild cabbage have lost the ability to be perennial, there are just a few forms where the perennial tendency has been increased. One worth considering is the TREE COLLARDS. This plant grows about 2 metres tall and wide, living for up to 20 years. It has mild flavoured dark green leaves that are wrinkled and look rather like Savoy cabbage leaves, though the plant does not form a heart. You harvest the young shoots when 5 - 25cm long and cook them stem and all. They are an excellent cabbage substitute.

A variety of KALE called Daubenton is another very good perennial form. About the same size as the preceding species, the leaves have a somewhat coarser flavour but make a very acceptable cooked vegetable.

Bunias orientalis

TURKISH ROCKET grows into a clump about 75cm tall and wide. It is a very easily grown plant, succeeding in most soils and preferring a sunny position, though It can also succeed in the light shade of a woodland garden. The plants are also tolerant of considerable neglect and, once established, will grow quite well even in long grass.

The young leaves have a mild flavour that is a cross between cabbage and radish. They go very well in a mixed salad and when cooked make an excellent vegetable. They are available early in the year, usually towards the end of winter, and the plant will continue to produce leaves until late autumn, with a bit of a gap when the plant is in flower.

Campanula species

This is a very large genus that contains some very desirable ornamental plants. They are in general fairly easy to grow, most of them preferring a position in full sun and all of them requiring a well-drained soil. They are little bothered by pests and diseases, though slugs adore the leaves and can

22 *Plants For A Future: www.pfaf.org*

totally decimate the plants in wet weather.

All members of this genus have more or less edible leaves, and some of them have such nice tasting leaves that it is surprising they are not better known. Only a few favourites are mentioned here, though feel free to try any other species you might be growing since none of them are poisonous.

C. persicifolia. This species grows about 1 metre tall, spreading quite quickly at the roots to form large clumps. It does well in light shade as well as full sun, growing well on a woodland edge. The leaves are rather narrow but have a pleasant slightly sweet flavour that can be used in salads. In mild winters, or when given the protection of a woodland, the plants will often produce leaves in the winter and can therefore be harvested all year round. The sub-species C. persicifolia crystalocalyx has larger leaves than the species and so is more suitable as a food crop.

C. poscharskyana. This is a low-growing evergreen plant. About 20cm tall, it spreads rapidly at the roots to form large clumps and therefore makes an excellent ground cover in a sunny position or light shade. Very tolerant of dry conditions, it will even succeed on an old brick wall. The leaves have a slightly sweet flavour, but are a bit on the chewy side. They provide a good source of winter leaves. and are an acceptable addition to mixed salads.

C. portenschlagiana is rather similar to the above and can be used in the same ways.

C. takesimana. Growing about 50cm tall and spreading rapidly at the roots, the leaves and leaf stems of this plant have a very similar flavour to iceberg lettuce. They are available from early spring until the autumn, though they can become a bit bitter in the summer.

C. versicolor. Growing up to 1.2 metres tall, this is an excellent salad plant. The leaves have a delicious sweetness that is very similar to fresh garden peas. The plants have a tap root and do not spread. They form a basal rosette of leaves in the winter and can be harvested in moderation in mild winters, and then in greater quantities in the spring and summer. Unfortunately, the plant is only hardy in milder areas and is not very productive of leaves. It is also very susceptible to attacks by slugs. However, if you want to give it a bit of extra care, it will reward you with some very tasty salads and also a superb display of flowers from mid summer until well into the autumn.

Cichorium intybus

CHICORY forms a rosette of leaves up to 50cm tall, though when flowering it sends up a shoot that can be 1.5 metres tall. It prefers growing in a sunny position and will succeed in any moderately fertile well-drained moisture retentive soil,

though it is most at home in chalky soils.

Chicory leaves are quite bitter, and few people can eat them in quantity. However, they are very nutritious and are especially beneficial to the healthy functioning of the liver and kidneys. Perhaps the best way of eating them is to chop them quite finely and use them as a minor ingredient of mixed salads that also contain some of the sweeter tasting leaves - this way you get their health benefits without really noticing the bitterness. Chicory is one of the most productive and reliable winter salad crops, though unfortunately you have to sow the seed of selected cultivars each year in order to produce winter leaves - see the section Winter Salads for more information on this.

Hibiscus syriacus

The ROSE OF SHARON is a deciduous shrub that grows up to 3 metres tall and 2 metres wide, though it can be kept smaller by trimming it, and can be grown as a hedge. It prefers a well-drained humus rich fertile soil in a sheltered position in full sun and succeeds in any soil of good or moderate quality. Plants are hardy to about -20°c but plants only really succeed in the warmer areas because of their late flowering habit. They are also slightly tender when young and when planted in colder areas, they will need protection for the first few winters.

The young leaves can be eaten raw or cooked. They have a very mild, slightly nutty flavour, and though slightly on the tough side they make an acceptable addition to the salad bowl.

Malva moschata

The MUSK MALLOW is a very easily grown plant that succeeds in most soils, though it prefers a reasonably well-drained and moderately fertile soil in a sunny position.

The leaves are available from early or mid spring until the plant comes into flower in the summer. If the plants are then trimmed back, they will produce a fresh flush of leaves in late summer and the early autumn. The leaves have a pleasant mild flavour with a mucilaginous texture that is very beneficial to the digestive system. These leaves can be used in bulk in salads, and they make an excellent lettuce substitute.

M. alcea is a closely related species that can be used similarly.

Montia perfoliata (Claytonia perfoliata)

MINER S LETTUCE is a short-lived annual to perennial plant, but it self-sows so freely that you will never be without it.

Edible Plants 23

Growing about 15cm tall, it usually forms a carpet of growth and makes a good ground cover. It prefers a moist peaty soil, though it can succeed on very poor and dry soils and thrives in the shade of trees. The leaves have a fairly bland flavour with a mucilaginous texture; they make a very acceptable salad and are available all year round, even in severe winters.

M. sibirica is a closely related species. It is more reliably perennial and can even succeed in the dense shade of beech trees. The leaves have a stronger flavour, with a distinct earthy taste of raw beetroot that not everyone likes.

Myrrhis odorata

SWEET CICELY grows up to 1 metre tall and wide. It prefers a moist rich soil in a shady position and grows very well on a woodland edge. The leaves have a delicious sweet aniseed flavour and make an excellent addition to mixed salads. They are also used as a flavouring for vegetables and can be cooked with tart fruits in order to reduce their acidity. The plant produces fresh leaves from late winter until early the following winter.

Oxalis deppei

The IRON CROSS PLANT is a very attractive bulbous plant that forms a fountain of leaves and flowers about 25cm tall and 15cm wide. Easily grown, it prefers a sandy soil in a warm dry sunny position and dislikes dry or heavy soils. It is only hardy outdoors in the milder temperate areas, tolerating temperatures down to about -5 c or perhaps a bit lower if the soil is very well-drained. The bulbs are easily harvested in late autumn, however, and can be stored overwinter in a cool frost free place, replanting them in the spring. In milder winter areas a good mulch is usually sufficient to see the bulbs through the winter and they will then normally be more productive of leaves and flowers in the following year. The leaves are available from late spring until the autumn frosts. They have a delicious lemony flavour and make an excellent flavouring in salads

Peltaria alliacea

GARLIC CRESS is a vigorous spreading plant that grows up to 30cm tall and makes a good ground cover in a sunny position or in light shade. It prefers a light fertile moist soil though it is not too fussy.

An evergreen plant, it provides its edible leaves all year round apart for a few weeks in the summer when it is flowering and producing seed. These leaves have a strong garlic/mustard flavour which make an excellent addition to salads or cooked dishes. They do develop a rather bitter aftertaste in hot dry weather, though.

Reichardia picroides

Looking somewhat like a dandelion, this plant grows about 30cm tall and wide, forming a basal rosette of leaves. It is easily grown in any moderately fertile well-drained soil in a sunny position, though it grows best in a shady position in summer where it will produce better quality leaves. It is not hardy in the colder areas of the country, tolerating temperatures down to between -5 and -10 c. It is likely to be hardier when grown in a soil on the poor side, though the leaves will not be so tender nor so freely produced. Plants are also likely to be hardier in well-drained soils and they dislike very wet weather. Ken Fern found this plant to be almost totally slug-proof, even in a very heavily slug-infested garden.

The leaves have a pleasant agreeable flavour with a slight sweetness; they make a very acceptable lettuce substitute. Unlike most salad plants, the older leaves often have a sweeter and more pleasant flavour than the young ones and remain sweet even when the plant is in flower. Cut the plant back regularly in the summer in order to produce fresh crops of leaves and make harvesting easier. In areas with mild winters the plant will provide edible leaves all year round.

Rumex acetosa

SORREL is a very easily grown and tolerant plant that can be up to 50cm tall and 30cm wide. It succeeds in most soils though it prefers a moist moderately fertile well-drained soil in a sunny position. Established plants are tolerant of considerable neglect, surviving and producing tasty leaves even in dense weed growth. They will also grow well in the sunnier areas of a woodland garden.

The leaves have a delicious acid flavour, they make a marvellous flavouring in mixed salads and can also be cooked like spinach. They can be munched on when working in the garden, as they have a very refreshing effect on the mouth and also relieve thirst. There are some named varieties of this species that have been selected for their larger leaves and reluctance to flower. For example, Ken Fern grew a Polish form that only flowered once in seven years, and produced masses of large leaves, with a small crop of smaller leaves all through the winter.

Rumex scutatus

FRENCH SORREL has a similar taste to the above, though is perhaps more delicate. Another very productive plant, though the leaves are rather smaller. It is a very drought tolerant plant and can even be grown in old walls.

Taraxacum officinale

The DANDELION is a common weed of lawns, growing about 30cm tall and producing a mass of attractive flowers in the spring. A very easily grown plant, it succeeds in most soils, though it prefers a well-drained humus-rich neutral to alkaline soil in full sun or light shade.

Like the chicory mentioned earlier, dandelion leaves are rather bitter but are an extremely healthy addition to the diet. If chopped and added in small quantities to mixed salads their bitterness is not overpowering. The easiest way of growing dandelions is to just allow them to look after themselves in the lawn. Not only will they provide you with edible leaves all year round, but they will also make the lawn look really pretty when they are flowering in the spring. There are also some cultivated forms of dandelion that are supposed to have better tasting leaves, though this is a matter of opinion.

Tilia cordata

The LIME TREE prefers a good moist loamy alkaline to neutral soil but it also succeeds on slightly acid soils. Growth is rather poor, however, if the soil is very dry or very wet. The plant tolerates considerable exposure to the wind and succeeds in sun or semi-shade.

The young leaves have a mild, slightly sweet taste with a somewhat mucilaginous texture. They make an excellent salad or sandwich filling and can be used in quantity when available. Lime trees usually produce a mass of young shoots from the base of their trunks and it is often possible to harvest these leaves from the middle of spring until early autumn.

One problem with growing this tree is that the leaves are very attractive to leaf aphis. These aphis produce an abundance of sweet secretions which drip off the leaves to the ground below and also attract sooty mould fungus. Any plants growing below a lime tree are likely to become covered with this mould.

All the other members of this genus also produce edible leaves -though some are rather on the tough side. We would most recommend our other two native species, T. platyphyllos and T. x vulgaris.

Urtica dioica

STINGING NETTLES are an excellent and nutritious cooked vegetable. They can usually be found growing luxuriantly in the wild, so there is little or no need to cultivate them. If you do want to grow them - and they are excellent plants for the wildlife garden as well as having a whole catalogue of other uses - then they prefer a soil rich in phosphates and nitrogen.

The young leaves make a very good spinach substitute and are also used for making soups. But they do smell rather like fish when they are cooking, which some may find unpleasant. Nettles are a very nutritious food that is easily digested and is high in minerals (especially iron) and vitamins (especially A and C). Only use the young leaves since old leaves can cause kidney upsets, and always wear stout gloves when harvesting them to prevent being stung. Cooking the leaves, or thoroughly drying them, completely neutralises the sting, rendering the leaf safe to eat.

Edible Plants **25**

Campanula species

Malva moschata MUSK MALLOW

Claytonia perfoliata MINER'S LETTUCE

Rumex scutatus FRENCH SORREL

Rumex acetosa SORREL

Taraxacum officinale DANDELION

Peltaria alliacea GARLIC CRESS

Reichardia picroides

Agastache foeniculum ANISE HYSSOP

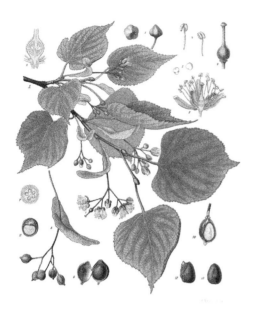
Tilia cordata LIME TREE

Urtica dioica STINGING NETTLES

Bunias orientalis TURKISH ROCKET

Myrrhis odorata

Hibiscus syriacus ROSE OF SHARON

Cichorium intybus CHICORY

Atriplex halimus SALT BUSH

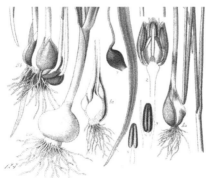
Allium species

Brassica oleracea

Edible Plants **27**

Edible Flowers

Many people find the concept of eating flowers to be a little strange - indeed there are a few who find the very idea to be distasteful. This is rather sad because, as well as providing a nutritious food, there are some amazing taste treats in store for those who are willing to experiment with their foods. Nutritionally, the flower can be divided into three main elements. Firstly, there is the pollen. Although only present in fairly small quantities, this is a very rich source of protein and so helps to build and maintain the body structure. Its flavour is usually rather bland. Secondly, we have the nectar. This is usually rather sweet and is the substance that most attracts bees to the flowers to pollinate them. The bees turn the nectar into honey - when we eat the flowers we can use the sugars in the nectar to provide us with a good source of energy. Nectar provides a balanced form of sugars together with a range of minerals and does not have the negative effects of refined sugars, such as rotting the teeth. Finally, we have the petals and other parts of the flower structure. Although not normally as nutritious as leaves, they do have many similarities nutritionally and so can provide us with a good range of vitamins and minerals. Yellow flowers, in particular, are very good sources of vitamin A.

The flavour and texture of flowers varies from species to species. Some are very crisp and crunchy, others almost silky soft. A few flowers have a very savoury taste whilst others can be very hot or have a very mild flavour. Depending on the quantities of nectar present, they can also be very sweet. If looking primarily for sweetness, by the way, you will normally be best off picking the flowers in the morning before bees and other insects have depleted the stocks of nectar.

Flowers can make a very attractive addition to salads, the only problem can be that they make a salad so attractive that people are reluctant to disturb what they see as a work of art! Flowers can also provide a tasty and thirst-quenching snack when working in the garden. In every case they are probably only suitable for eating raw, as they are so delicate that both their texture and taste would be destroyed by cooking. Unless stated otherwise, all the plants listed below are herbaceous perennials and should be hardy in most parts of the country. They are quite a diverse range of plants, and species suitable for almost any niche in the garden will be found here. It is therefore very difficult to give general notes on their cultivation needs, though a very brief guide will be given.

Allium species

The flowers of the various ONIONS and GARLICS have a very similar taste to the leaves, though they are usually somewhat stronger and also sweeter. They make a particularly attractive addition to salads. By careful selection of species, it is possible to have flowers from spring to early winter. Please see the pfaf.org website for Allium species -the Perennial Onions , which deals with this genus in much greater detail than can be covered here. Unless stated otherwise, all members of this genus require a well-drained soil and a sunny position. In general they do not grow well with weed competition, though there are exceptions.

A. cernuum. The NODDING ONION grows about 40cm tall, forming a clump about 25cm wide, it has some of the most beautiful flowers in the genus. These are produced in mid summer and have a strong onion flavour. If you can obtain it, the cultivar Major is a more vigorous form with larger flower clusters.

A. moly. GOLDEN GARLIC grows up to 30cm tall and 10cm wide. Its yellow flowers are produced in early summer and have a very crisp texture with a garlic-like flavour. An excellent flavouring in salads, though too strong to be used in large quantities. Be careful not to get the sub-species A. moly bulbiferum since this produces bulbils in the flowering head and can be invasive. Golden garlic is a very vigorous plant that can look after itself, it is useful for naturalising between shrubs and grows well at the base of a beech hedge in a wet garden.

A. neapolitanum. Growing up to 30cm tall and 20cm wide, DAFFODIL GARLIC produces its white flowers in mid spring. These have a delicious sweetness followed by a fairly strong garlic flavour. The plant is not hardy in the colder areas, but in gardens where it is happy it will usually self-sow quite freely. Try to obtain the cultivar 'Grandiflorum' since this has larger flowers which are also produced in greater abundance.

A. tuberosum. GARLIC CHIVES grows about 30cm tall and 25cm wide. Its white flowers, which are produced in the autumn, have a pleasant onion flavour.

A. ursinum. WILD GARLIC is a plant for naturalising in woodlands, where it can form extensive carpets of growth. The white flowers are produced in mid to late spring and have a strong garlic flavour.

Aquilegia vulgaris.

COLUMBINE is a very beautiful British native plant growing up to 1 metre tall and 50cm wide. Very easily grown, it succeeds in most soils and prefers a position in sun or light shade. When well sited it will usually self-sow freely. Although all other parts of the plant are mildly toxic, the flowers are perfectly safe to eat. Rich in nectar, they make a sweet and delightful addition to mixed salads. There are many named varieties and a whole range of different colours can be grown. All other members of this genus can be used in similar ways.

Asclepias tuberosa

Growing up to 75cm tall and 50cm wide, PLEURISY ROOT prefers a well-drained light, rich or peaty soil that is on the dry side, and a sunny position. The plants are particularly attractive to slugs and some protection will probably be required, especially in the spring when the new shoots come into growth. The beautiful orange flowers are produced in mid to late summer. In hot weather they produce so much nectar that this crystallises out into small lumps which can then be eaten like sweets. The flower clusters can also be boiled down to make a sugary syrup. For more information about the many uses of this plant and other members of the genus, please see the pfaf.org website for The Milkweeds .

Asphodeline lutea

Growing up to 1 metre tall and eventually forming a clump 1 metre or more wide, YELLOW ASPHODEL is a very easily grown plant that succeeds in most soils so long as they are well drained. It grows best in full sun, though it also tolerates partial shade and is very drought tolerant. The yellow star-shaped flowers are an epicurean's treat. They have a delightful sweetness and are delicious either on their own or in salads. They do need to be used as soon as possible after harvesting, however, because they do not store and will soon start to decompose. The plant flowers from late spring until the middle of summer -individual flowers are very short-lived, but new flowers are produced every day. If you pick them in the evening you can enjoy them visually during the day and gastronomically in the evening.

Campanula species

This is a very large genus that contains some very desirable ornamental plants. They are in general fairly easy to grow, most of them preferring a position in full sun and all of them requiring a well-drained soil. They are little bothered by pests and diseases, though slugs adore the leaves and can totally decimate the plants in wet weather. All members of this genus have more or less edible flowers; these are usually bell-shaped and come in some shade of blue, though whites can often also be found. They usually have a mild flavour with a delicate sweetness. Only two favourites are mentioned here, though feel free to try any other species you might be growing since none of them are poisonous.

C. persicifolia. This species grows about 1 metre tall,

spreading quite quickly at the roots to form large clumps. It succeeds in light shade or full sun, growing well on a woodland edge. The flowers are produced from early to mid summer.

C. versicolor. Growing up to 1.2 metres tall and 50cm wide, the beautiful flowers are produced in abundance from mid summer, until the autumn frosts finally convince the plant that no more seed will be ripened this year. The plant requires a warm, sheltered position and is not hardy in the colder areas.

Cercis siliquastrum

The JUDAS TREE is a deciduous tree growing up to 12 metres tall and 10 metres wide, though it is usually somewhat smaller in temperate regions. It succeeds in most soils, including chalk and dry sands, though it dislikes growing in wet soils, especially when these are of clay. A nitrogen-fixing plant, it flowers better, and is somewhat hardier, when growing on a poorish soil. It requires a very warm sunny position if it is to flower well. The purple pea-like flowers are produced on the branches of the previous or earlier years, and also on the trunk of the plant. They have a sweetish-acid taste and are a nice addition to the salad bowl.

Feijoa sellowiana /Acca sellowiana

The FEIJOA is an evergreen shrub growing up to 3 metres tall and wide, though it can be kept smaller by trimming. It is not very cold hardy and needs the protection of a sunny south or west-facing wall in all but the mildest areas. It prefers a light loamy well-drained soil and can tolerate drought and salt winds. The flower petals are thick and crunchy with a sweet, crisp and delicious flavour, indeed they taste more like a fruit than many fruits.

Hemerocallis species

DAYLILIES are commonly grown ornamental plants. Easily cultivated, they grow well in most soils, though they do best in rich moist conditions and succeed in sun or shade. They are very tolerant of neglect and will succeed in short grass if the soil is moist. The only real difficulty in growing the plants is that slugs really adore the young growth and can cause considerable damage to newly planted plants or the young growth in spring. All members of this genus have edible flowers. These are trumpet-shaped, vary in size from 5 - 20cm. and look like lilies. In most of the species these flowers only live for one day, hence the common name. The petals are crisp and juicy with a mild sweet flavour - the base of the flower is particularly sweet due to the nectar contained there - and they make an excellent munch in the garden or can be used to decorate salads. In China the flowers are harvested as they begin to wither and are then dried and used as a flavouring and thickener in cooked foods. The following species are amongst our favourites, though it is also worthwhile trying any of the many cultivars that are grown. The only word of warning is that if the flowers are bright yellow or scented then they can often have an unpleasant aftertaste. For more information on this genus please see the pfaf.org website for 'Hemerocallis Species - The Day Lilies'.

H. dumortieri. The plants grow about 45cm tall and form a tight slowly-spreading clump 60cm or more wide. They flower from late spring to early summer.

H. fulva. If you are only going to grow one daylily, then this is the species to go for. A vigorous spreading plant, it grows up to 1 metre tall and 1 metre or more wide. The flowers can be up to 20cm long, they have particularly thick, crunchy and tasty petals, whilst the taste is just amazing. They are produced in mid-summer. There are a number of double-flowered named cultivars of this species that are cultivated for their edible flowers in the Orient. With twice as many petals per flower, these are especially delicious to eat. Cultivars to look out for are Kwanzo , Green Kwanzo and Flore pleno .

H. middendorffii esculenta grows about 50cm tall and wide, flowering in early to mid summer. The flowers are up to 10cm long and are another of the especially well flavoured ones.

H. multiflora. Growing up to 1 metre tall and forming a tight clump about 60cm or more wide, the flowers of this species are only about 5 - 8cm long but are produced in great profusion from mid to late summer.

Hibiscus syriacus

A deciduous shrub growing up to 3 metres tall and 2 metres wide, though it can be kept smaller by trimming. It succeeds in any soil of good or moderate quality, though it prefers a well-drained humus rich fertile soil and a sheltered position in full sun. It dislikes deep shade or badly drained soils and grows best with its roots in cool moist soil and its tops in a hot sunny position. Although hardy to about -20°c, it flowers in the autumn and will only produce these flowers in profusion when growing in warmer temperate areas. The flowers are 5cm or more across and are stunningly beautiful - there are many named varieties providing a wide range of colours. The flavour is mild and they have a mucilaginous texture. They are delightful in salads, both for looking at and for eating.

Malva moschata

The MUSK MALLOW is another very easily grown plant, growing up to 80cm tall and 60cm wide. It succeeds in most soils, though it prefers a reasonably well-drained and moderately fertile soil in a sunny position. Individual plants

are generally quite short-lived though they can self-sow freely when in a suitable position and usually more than maintain themselves. The flowers are produced in great abundance in mid summer - if the plants are cut back when they are finishing flowering then they will often produce a fresh flush in early spring. These flowers have a very mild flavour and mucilaginous texture; they make an excellent and very decorative addition to the salad bowl. M. alcea is a closely related plant that can be used in the same way.

Oxalis deppei

The IRON CROSS PLANT is a dainty creature that grows up to 30cm tall and 10cm wide. An easily grown plant, it prefers a well-drained sandy soil in a warm dry position and strongly dislikes wet or heavy soils. It is only hardy outdoors in the milder areas, tolerating temperatures down to about -5 c, or perhaps a bit lower if the soil is very well-drained. The bulbs are easily harvested in late autumn, however, and can be stored overwinter in a cool frost free place, replanting them in the spring. In milder winter areas a good mulch is usually sufficient to see the bulbs through the winter and they will then normally be more productive of leaves and flowers in the following year. The flowers are produced from early or mid-summer until growth is killed back by autumn frosts.

These flowers have a delicious lemony flavour, they make a delightful thirst-quenching munch and are an excellent flavouring in salads. They do contain oxalic acid, however, and so should not be eaten in large quantities since they can prevent the body being able to absorb certain nutrients from food that is consumed with them. People with a tendency to rheumatism, arthritis, gout, kidney stones and hyperacidity should take special caution if including this plant in their diet since it can exacerbate their condition.

Ribes odoratum

A deciduous shrub growing about 2 metres tall and wide, the GOLDEN CURRANT is easily grown in a moisture retentive but well-drained loamy soil of at least moderate quality. It prefers full sun but is also quite tolerant of shade, though it does not fruit so well in such a position. It grows especially well on the sunny edges of woodland. A very ornamental plant, the attractive yellow flowers are produced in profusion in mid-spring and have a pleasant sweet taste. R. aureum is a very closely related species that can also be used.

Sambucus nigra

The ELDERBERRY is a deciduous shrub or small tree growing up to 6 metres tall and wide. Yet another very easily grown plant, it tolerates most soils and situations, growing well on chalk and in heavy clay soils. It tolerates some shade but

30 *Plants For A Future: **www.pfaf.org***

fruits better in a sunny position. It also tolerates atmospheric pollution and coastal situations. The small white flowers are produced in large racemes in late spring and early summer. They make a delicious refreshing snack on a hot day, though you have to be a bit careful when eating them because they are very attractive to a wide range of insects and you could end up eating more than you had bargained for. The flowers can also be used to add a muscatel flavour to stewed fruits, jellies and jams, and are often used to make a sparkling wine.

Tropaeolum majus

The only annual plant included in this section, the garden NASTURTIUM tolerates most soils, though it prefers a rich light well-drained soil in full sun or partial shade. More and lusher leaves are produced when the plant is growing in a rich soil, though less flowers are produced. When grown in a soil of low fertility the leaves are smaller and less lush, though more flowers are produced. Plants will often maintain themselves by self-sowing, though in cold springs the seed will often not germinate until mid or even late summer, which is too late to produce a reasonable crop. A very ornamental and free-flowering species, it is often in bloom from early summer until cut down by the autumn frosts. There are many named varieties, ranging from vigorous climbing forms to low-growing dwarf forms. The flowers have a hot, watercress-like flavour and make a tasty addition to the salad bowl. T. minus is a closely related species with the same uses.

Typha angustifolia

The REEDMACE is a very easily grown plant for boggy pond margins or shallow water up to 15cm deep. It requires a rich soil if it is to do well and succeeds in full sun or part shade. A very invasive plant, it grows 2 metres or more tall and spreads freely at the roots when in a suitable site. It is much too vigorous for growing in small areas and unless restrained by some means, such as a large bottomless container, the plant will soon completely take over a site and will grow into the pond, gradually filling it in. This species will often form an almost complete monoculture in boggy soil. The young flowering stems can be eaten raw, cooked or made into a soup. They have a taste like sweet corn.

Viola odorata

The SWEET VIOLET succeeds in most soils but prefers a cool moist well-drained humus-rich soil in partial or dappled shade and protection from scorching winds. When grown in an open sunny position it prefers a moderately heavy rich soil. Sweet violets are evergreen perennials growing about 15cm tall and forming spreading clumps. They make an excellent weed-excluding ground cover and will often self-sow when well sited. The delicately scented flowers are produced in late winter and early spring, at which time they are usually the only edible flower available. The flowers are usually deep blue in colour, though there are also white forms. Their sweetly perfumed taste makes them a treat not to be missed. They are also said to be useful as a thickener in soups and stews, and they are used fresh to flavour and colour confectionery. All other members of this genus have more or less edible flowers and are worth trying.

Yucca baccata

There are many hardy species of YUCCA and all of them have more or less edible flowers, though this species is perhaps the best to eat. They thrive in any soil that is very well-drained, but prefer a sandy loam and full exposure to the south. They require a hot dry position if they are to thrive and flower well, once established they are very drought resistant. They are also much hardier when grown on poor sandy soils. There is some disagreement over the hardiness of this species, with some reports saying that it is only hardy in milder areas and another saying that the plants are hardy to at least -30 c. It can be seen doing well in a number of gardens in southern Britain, and it has certainly survived temperatures down to at least -10°c. The white flowers are thick and crunchy with a sweet flavour. It is best to eat them after they have been open for a few days otherwise they can have a soapy flavour.

Edible Plants **31**

Cercis siliquastrum JUDAS TREE

Aquilegia vulgaris COLUMBINE

Asphodeline lutea

Sambucus nigra ELDERBERRY

Hemerocallis species DAYLILIES

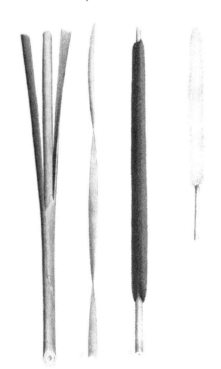
Typha angustifolia

Viola odorata SWEET VIOLET

Asclepias tuberosa PLEURISY ROOT

Feijoa sellowiana (Acca sellowiana)

32 Plants For A Future: *www.pfaf.org*

Tropaeolum majus NASTURTIUM *Ribes odoratum* GOLDEN CURRANT *Yucca baccata*

Edible Plants **33**

Winter Salads

Although it is relatively easy to grow leaves for winter consumption, most of the plants used in conventional gardening tend to be annuals (such as cabbage or spinach) and are also nicer when cooked. There are relatively few well known winter salad leaves and many of these (such as winter lettuce) require protection in all but mild winters. We would like to look at a few alternative winter salad plants and how they can be grown outdoors without protection to provide tasty salads throughout the winter. The milder the winters are in your area then the greater the variety that you will be able to grow, but this section contains plants suitable even for the coldest areas. Unless it says otherwise, all the plants are herbaceous perennials and do not need much work to maintain them once they are established. Many of them are also very ornamental and will not look at all out of place in the flower garden.

Spring to early summer is the best time to plan and plant out the garden. If done at this time of the year you will be able to harvest your leaves in the following winter. When deciding on the size of the garden it is important to remember that plant growth in the winter is much slower than in the summer. In general you need more plants to supply the same quantity of leaves. You also need to understand the growth habit of the plants you are growing. Some, such as chicory, do most of their growing in the summer and autumn; the leaves are hardy enough to stand up to the rigours of winter and can be harvested as required. The plants will make very little further growth until the warmer weather arrives. A few of the plants are evergreen; although they make very little growth in the winter they can be picked with care throughout this season. A number of other plants, usually from Mediterranean climates, have a dormant period in the summer (the dry season in the Mediterranean) and begin their growth cycle in the autumn. They grow slowly throughout the winter and can be harvested moderately as required. Finally, a number of plants come into new growth very early in the year and will normally provide good yields towards the end of winter.

The next step is to choose a suitable site for the garden. The primary requirements are:¬

1.   The site must be well-drained. Standing water is one of the biggest enemies of the winter garden.

2.   It must be in a sheltered position. It is especially important that the site is protected from cold winds (those from the north and north east in Britain).

3.   It should be at least fairly sunny. A position that is completely open to the south or southwest is best, southeast or west are the next best, other positions are not very suitable.

4.   The ground should be fertile, but not too rich. What is required is healthy growth but not luxuriant growth, since this is often soft and sappy and therefore more susceptible to damage by the cold.

Many of the plants in the list below can be easily obtained from a garden centre or as seed. The native species can be obtained from the wild (so long as you have the permission of the land owner!). Unless stated otherwise, the seed of all these plants can be sown in early spring in a greenhouse or cold frame. Prick the plants out into individual pots when they are large enough to handle and plant them into their permanent positions in early summer. Most of the perennials can be divided in the spring or autumn, but spring is usually best especially if you want to harvest them in the coming winter. The few shrubs in the list are easily increased by cuttings in mid-summer.

The next thing you need to do is to select the plants. The following list is far from exhaustive, but it does contain some of the more popular leaves grown and tried by Ken Fern in Cornwall.

Alliaria petiolata

Hedge garlic. This native biennial plant can be found wild in many hedgerows so there is probably little need to cultivate it. The leaves, flowers and young seedpods have a flavour that is somewhat like a cross between garlic and mustard -fairly pleasant when added in small quantities to a salad. This is one of the more shade-tolerant plants on the list. If you decide to cultivate it then collect the seeds from wild plants in early summer and sow them straightaway in situ. They will normally maintain themselves by self-sowing.

Allium species

Onions, Chives etc. There are a number of species in this genus that can supply winter leaves. The British native wild garlic, A. ursinum, is a woodland plant. Usually available from late winter, the leaves and flowers have a delicious mild garlic flavour. An aggressive spreader, it is probably best left in the woodland, it is also more tolerant of wet soils than other plants in this list. The leaves of A. neapolitanum, the daffodil garlic, are available all through the winter and the plant produces beautiful white flowers in early spring. Both the leaves and the flowers have a garlic flavour and are delightful in salads. Whilst seed of this plant can be sown in the spring, best results will be obtained by sowing it in a greenhouse in early autumn. This species is only hardy milder areas. The perennial onion, A. cepa Perutile is more reliable in colder areas - its mild onion flavoured leaves are available all year round. There are many other Allium species to choose from -the following should be hardy in most temperate regions. Welsh onions, A. fistulosum often die down in severe winters but will be back again in late winter. Chives, A. schoenoprasum, die down in early winter but are back in late winter too. The three-cornered leek, A. triquetrum can be available from autumn onwards and has naturalized in parts of Britain.

Atriplex halimus

The salt bush, is an evergreen shrub growing 1 metre or more tall. Very resistant to maritime exposure, it can be trimmed and grown as a hedge to provide shelter for other plants in the winter garden. The leaves are more silvery than green and have a distinctive salty flavour. It can be picked in moderation throughout the winter. It has become naturalized on the coasts of S. England but is not hardy in the colder areas of Britain. A. canescens is a very similar-looking N. American shrub that has the same uses.

Barbarea vulgaris

This plant is our native yellow rocket. A short-lived perennial growing about 30cm tall, it has a hot watercress-like flavour.

It might die down in colder winters and usually self-sows when happy. B. verna, American land cress, is related to this plant and can also be grown for winter salads, though it is not reliably perennial and is normally sown in late summer or early autumn in order to provide winter leaves.

Beta vulgaris cicla

B. vulgaris cicla is the cultivated spinach beet. Although it is a biennial, this plant usually self-sows freely and provides fresh leaves all year round with very little effort from the grower. The much more ornamental cultivar Ruby Chard can also be used but it does not self-sow as freely, nor is it so hardy, often dying down in cold winters. A good salad leaf, but with a raw beetroot-like flavour that is not to everyone's taste.

Campanula poscharskyana

C. poscharskyana is a lovely carpeting harebell (or bluebell if you live in Scotland). About 10 - 25cm tall, this is a rampantly spreading plant that makes good ground-cover. The leaves, although small, are a very nice mild salad and can be eaten all year round.

Campanula versicolor

It is about 1.2 metres tall and flowers in late summer. The

plant keeps a basal rosette of leaves all winter and, although

only growing slowly, it can be harvested in moderation all

through the winter. The leaves have a delicious sweet flavour and are one of the more popular salad leaves. The plant is not hardy in the colder areas and is also popular with slugs.

Cardamine hirsuta

Hairy bittercress is a common garden weed. The leaves have a hot cress-like flavour and, once you have the plant in your garden, it will normally self sow. The leaves are available all year round.

Cichorium intybus

Chicory is a fairly well known salad plant. Although a perennial, it is best to sow the seed annually in late spring or early summer for winter leaves. Older plants tend to die down in the winter or only produce a very small basal rosette. It is important to choose the correct cultivars - Sugar Loaf is one of the best. The leaves have a somewhat bitter taste that many people enjoy, they can be blanched to make them milder but this will be at the expense of many vitamins and minerals.

Claytonia virginica

Spring beauty is about 20cm tall and usually provides leaves throughout the winter. Both the leaves and the flowers can be eaten and have a fairly mild flavour. The taste is suggestive of raw beetroot, which not everybody enjoys.

Foeniculum vulgare

Very easy to grow, these fennel plants die down in mid-winter, but in mild areas start growing again almost immediately. In colder areas they will probably be somewhat later into growth. The leaves have an aniseed flavour. The plant is rather vigorous, growing about 1 metre tall and wide. It also self-sows freely.

Montia sibirica / Claytonia sibirica

Pink purslane is a short-lived perennial, but it self-sows freely and maintains itself so well that it can be used as a ground cover plant. Only about 10cm tall, it is evergreen and both the leaves and flowers can be eaten. A fairly bland flavour, though it becomes somewhat bitter in hot dry weather. M. perfoliata, the miner s lettuce, is an annual that self-sows freely and is also usually available all through the winter.

Both of these plants are extremely hardy, they are native to

Edible Plants **35**

Alaska and Siberia where they can be harvested from under the snow even in the depths of winter.

Myrrhis odorata

The British native Sweet Cicely has a delightful aniseed flavour and it goes very well as a flavouring in a mixed salad. It dies down in early winter but in mild areas it will grow again quickly and produce leaves even in mid-winter. The seed is said to have a short viability and is best sown as soon as it is ripe. A well-grown plant is about 1 metre tall and wide.

Peltaria alliacea

A very easily grown plant, it has a rather strong garlic/mustard flavour that some people adore in salads. It becomes much more bitter in the summer. An evergreen herb about 10cm tall it spreads freely once established.

Reichardia picroides

This plant looks somewhat similar to a dandelion but wait until you taste the leaves! Instead of the bitterness of a dandelion the leaves have a very acceptable flavour with a slight sweetness. They can be used in quantity in salads - far better than lettuce and so much easier to grow. It is one of the few plants we have where we like the leaves but the slugs don t. It really has rave reviews and is incredibly productive - even when the plants are flowering the leaves maintain their delicious flavour.

Rumex acetosa

Sorrel is an excellent salad plant. The leaves have a delicious lemon flavour, though they should not be eaten in quantity since they contain oxalic acid. Ken Fern has grown a very superior cultivar from Poland that virtually never flowers and provides large tasty leaves all the year round. Plants are about 40cm tall and spread slowly.

Rumex alpinus

Unlike other docks, the leaves of the alpine dock make a fairly acceptable addition to winter salads (and a delicious spinach substitute). The plant stays green all winter if the weather is mild, otherwise it will die down but reappear in late winter. The leaves become bitterer in the summer but are still acceptable cooked. A very vigorous plant, growing about 60cm tall and wide.

Sanguisorba minor

Salad burnet is an evergreen British native plant that is sometimes cultivated for its edible leaves. Very easy to grow and often self-sowing freely, the leaves can be eaten all year round and some people claim that they have the flavour of cucumbers, but not everyone likes them. Plants are about 50cm tall when flowering and 30cm wide.

Smyrnium olusatrum

Alexanders grows wild in hedgerows in many parts of Britain and does not really need to be cultivated. The leaves have a strong celery-like flavour and are not to everyone's taste. A biennial, it grows about 1 metre tall and self-sows freely if given a suitable position.

Taraxacum officinale

Nutritionally very valuable, many people find dandelions too bitter for salads. However, the winter leaves are less bitter and a few leaves added to a chopped salad will hardly be noticed. There are also some cultivated forms that are said to have nicer tasting leaves, but you may not notice the difference. The seed can be obtained from some of the larger seed catalogues. It is probably easier to grow this plant in the lawn - if you let the grass grow a little longer in the winter it will protect the dandelions and they will then be more productive as well as more tender. There are also a number of dandelion look-alikes that can be found growing in gardens and hedgerows in the winter.

Thymus vulgaris

The garden thyme is a dwarf evergreen shrub, usually less than 30cm tall. T. Vulgaris is an excellent addition to salads adding a delightful fragrance. It has also been shown that eating thyme daily can prolong active life.

Valerianella locusta.

Corn salad is a British native annual that is sometimes cultivated for its mild-tasting leaves. If allowed to flower it will usually self-sow and can then be available all year round. .

Viola odorata.

Sweet violets are about 10cm tall and come into flower in the depths of winter. Both the leaves and the flowers can be added to salads, they have a fairly bland flavour, the flowers doing wonders to brighten up winter salads.

Valerianella locusta CORN SALAD

Thymus vulgaris GARDEN THYME

Smyrnium olusatrum ALEXANDERS

Sanguisorba minor SALAD BURNET

Rumex alpinus

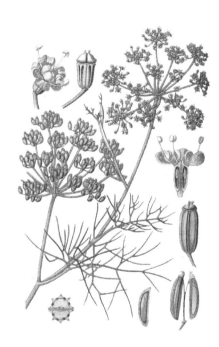
Foeniculum vulgare

Campanula poscharskyana HAREBELL

Claytonia virginica

SALT BUSH

Edible Plants 37

Claytonia sibirica PINK PURSLANE

C. hirsuta HAIRY BITTERCRESS

Campanula versicolor

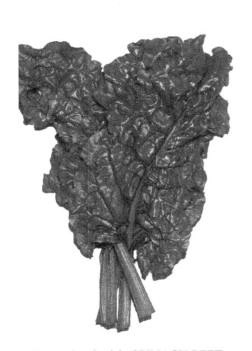
Beta vulgaris cicla SPINACH BEET

Barbarea vulgaris YELLOW ROCKET

Alliaria petiolata HEDGE GARLIC

38 Plants For A Future: www.pfaf.org

Staple seed crops from perennials

 Yes, alright, you do grow lots of different tasting fruits, flowers and leaves, but what about real foods? - something that will fill me up. You don't seem to grow any staple foods here! Whilst it is possible to get good crops of leaves from perennial plants within a year or two of moving onto a new site, and there are several fruits that can yield within a few years, obtaining staple foods such as nuts, legumes and cereals from perennials can take considerably longer. It can take 30 - 40 years before some nut trees start to produce useful yields. There is also very little information about the potential of perennials to produce worthwhile crops in temperate climates.

Never the less, there are quite a number of species that can be grown with the confidence that in time they will provide good and reliable crops. Before looking at these, however, we would like to mention a few annual plants that can be used to fill the gap between planting the trees and obtaining a crop from them.

Quinoa, Chenopodium quinoa is a plant that is becoming much better known. Related to the British native weed fat hen, it produces good yields of very nutritious seeds that are a good source of a high quality protein and can be used in all the ways that rice is used.

There are several legumes that yield good crops. The most reliable must be broad beans, Vicia faba, but French beans, Phaseolus vulgaris, can also produce good crops of seed in warm summers. One exciting potential crop for temperate regions is a lupin from S. America - Lupinus mutabilis is nutritionally very similar to soya beans but easier to grow and higher yielding in this country. Most forms have bitter tasting seeds, this bitterness can be removed by soaking the seed for 12 -24 hours and changing the water 2 or 3 times. There are some varieties being developed that have sweet tasting seeds. Runner beans, Phaseolus coccineus, are perennials, the roots are hardy to about -5 c and if mulched will survive the winter in many areas. Yields, however, are lower in succeeding years than in the first year. There are also the various cultivated cereals such as wheat, oats, barley and rye.

Nut trees

There are quite a number of potentially high-cropping nut trees that can be grown in temperate regions, but this section focuses on those considered most likely to produce good yields. Therefore almonds, Prunus dulcis, must be discounted, as they flower much too early and rarely yield well.

Juglans regia

Walnuts can give good yields but this crop is also unpredictable. But since walnut trees have so many other uses, anyone with enough land should seriously consider a small walnut plantation. (1) The sap can be tapped in spring and used to make a sugar. (2) A wide range of dyes can be obtained from various parts of the plant. (3) An edible oil from the seed can also be used in soap making, paints, etc (though it quickly goes rancid). (4) The nuts can be used as a wood polish - simply crack open the shell and rub the kernel into the wood to release the oils then wipe off with a clean cloth. (5) The dried fruit rind is used to paint doors, window frames etc (it probably protects the wood due to its tannin content). (6) The crushed leaves are an insect repellent; a substance called juglone is secreted from the roots of this tree, it has an inhibitory effect on the growth of many other plants. (7) The fresh or dried bark of the tree and the fruit rind can be dried and used as a tooth cleaner. (8) The wood is a very valuable timber and is used for furniture making, veneer etc. With all these other uses, what does it matter if you don t get nuts every year!

There are many named forms of Cob-nuts and Filberts, Corylus avellana and C. maxima (derived in part from the British native hazel) and these are a good staple to grow. Even these can be unpredictable because of the earliness of their flowering. They are relatively quick to come into bearing however, and usually give good yields.

Araucaria araucana

One very good and reliable cropper, especially in the western part of Britain, is Araucaria araucana, the Monkey-puzzle tree. This tree comes from S. America and the seed is a staple crop of the native Indians. Research carried out in the 1800 s suggested that this tree is potentially heavier yielding in Britain than the native hazel. The seed is about the size of an almond; it is rich in fat and has a nice mild nutty flavour. It is produced in a cone about the size of a person s head, each cone contains up to 200 seeds. Some reports say that the cone falls to the ground with the seeds inside it; others say that the seed is shed from the cone whilst still on the tree. A very wind- resistant tree, tolerating maritime exposure, it casts little shade and so can be used as the top storey of a forest garden. There are some drawbacks - it takes up to 40 years from seed before it comes into bearing and you need to grow at least one male tree for every 5 -6 females in order to get seed but unfortunately it is impossible to distinguish males from females until they flower. However, there is a means of taking cuttings by using small adventitious growths that are sometimes found growing out of the trunk and so it is possible to obtain plants of known sex. It is also possible that these cuttings will fruit more quickly than seedlings. More research is needed into this subject.

Edible Plants **39**

Cephalotaxus harringtonii

C. harringtonii and C. fortunei are small conifers that look rather like the British native yew (Taxus baccata), and crop well almost every year in the right conditions. The seed is a little smaller than an almond and is contained in a thick fleshy 'fruit' (botanically called an aril). This seed is eaten in Asia but is bitter unless fully ripe, and even then is probably best cooked. The fruit, when fully ripe, is sweet and quite pleasant to eat, unripe it tastes like turpentine! The plants are very shade-tolerant (they have been seen carrying a heavy crop when growing in the quite dense shade of other conifers). They require a shady position if they are to do well when grown in the sunnier and warmer areas, though they succeed in a sunny position in the sheltered valleys of Scotland. They are quite slow growing and you need to grow at least one male plant for every 5 - 6 females.

Torreya nucifera

Another coniferous nut tree worthy of attention is Torreya nucifera. This plant is a staple crop in parts of China, the pleasantly flavoured seed is slightly larger than an almond and it seems regularly to produce good crops. The fruit looks very similar to Cephalotaxus species, but it is not edible. The tree grows well in light shade.

Castanea sativa

The sweet chestnut, grows and fruits very well in temperate regions, though unfortunately the climate is not always warm enough to produce the best quality large seeds. Even if the seed is somewhat smaller than the ones you can buy in the shops, the flavour is the same and overall yields are usually good. It is a very large tree, however, and is not the sort of thing you would want in your average back garden.

C. pumila, the Chinquapin, might be an answer here, only growing about 3.5 metres tall and wide. The books say that it does not fruit in Britain, but some trees in S England have been seen to produce crops from time to time. The seed is rather small, but it is well flavoured. The chinquapin is a very good plant to grow in the light shade of pine trees, succeeding in sandy acid soils. Whereas most nut seeds are rich in fats, this genus produces seeds rich in carbohydrates, and they can be used as an alternative to cereals in the diet.

Quercus ilex

The holm oak, grows well in most parts of Britain and other temperate regions. A large spreading evergreen tree, it can also be trimmed and used as a hedge, though it is unlikely to produce many of its edible seeds when grown this way. Very resistant to maritime exposure, it is often used to provide shelter in the windy gardens of Cornwall The seed is similar to, but smaller than, the British native oak and can be used in the same ways as sweet chestnuts (to which it is nutritionally similar). Trees usually fruit abundantly, the quality of the seed varies from tree to tree, and the best are free of any bitterness and can be eaten raw or cooked. The sub-species Q. ilex ballota used to be cultivated as a food crop in Spain and Portugal.

Cereals

There are many more nut trees with potential for temperate regions, but when it comes to perennial cereals and pulses the choice is more restricted. Most perennial cereals tend to have one or more of the following drawbacks:- low yields, small seeds, difficult to extract. There is some research being carried out in N. America, but this is looking mainly at crops for arid areas and is not so relevant. Because crops are normally obtained in their first or second years growth, there is a large potential for selective breeding in order to produce more productive perennial cereals. The authors only know of one species that has produced well. This is Secale montana a perennial rye that is believed to be the parent of the cultivated cereal rye, though the seed is somewhat smaller. Ken Fern s experience was that this cropped well despite considerable neglect; yields were fair though much less than from the annual rye.

Beckmannia eruciformis

B. eruciformis grows wild in swamps and shallow water, though it will tolerate drier soils, it also succeeds in saline soils. Plants can grow up to 1.5 metres tall but are much smaller in drier soils. The seed is very small but is easy to harvest and produced in abundance. It probably has the potential for improvement and has been used in the past for making bread.

Glyceria fluitans

Floating manna grass grows best in shallow slow-flowing or stagnant water, though it also succeeds in wet soils. It is about 50cm tall. Its rather small seed can be eaten raw or cooked and has a sweetish taste. The plant has occasionally been cultivated for its seed; this is considered a delicacy in some parts of Europe and was an article of commerce until well into the 20th century. Flour from the seed is said to make bread that is a little inferior to wheat bread, the flour can also be used as a thickener in soups etc. when it imparts a sweet, delicate flavour.

Triticum aestivum

Wheat has a potential to perennate and there is at least one cultivar, called appropriately enough Perennial that has been selected for this trait. It is said to yield well, though only a proportion of the plants live for a second or third year, however, and very few live longer than this. At present we feel that the oak and chestnuts mentioned above are the best substitutes for cereals, though they cannot be used in all the same ways as cereals.

Legumes

The situation with peas and beans is somewhat more promising.

Caragana species

There are a number of Caragana species, in particular C. arborescens, the Siberian pea shrub, that can yield good crops of edible seeds. The seed is about the size of a lentil and is somewhat tedious to harvest, but that can be tolerated since it is about the only thing you will have to do to the plant. This seed is very nutritious, containing about 12% fat and 36% protein. Although there have been suggestions that the seed contains toxic substances, this has been discounted in more recent studies. C. boisii and C. fruticosa are closely related to this species and can probably be used in a similar way. C. brevispina has somewhat larger seeds, though these are more bitter than C. arborescens. Caraganas come from climates with much colder winters than most temperate regions, but also with hotter summers, they therefore grow and fruit better under these conditions. They do not really like very humid climates. Give them as sunny a position as possible and a well-drained soil. They are fairly fast growing, tolerate drought and poor soils, C. arborescens also succeeds in very alkaline soils.

Desmanthus illinoensis

D. illinoensis is a N. American perennial that is being evaluated by the Land Institute of Salina, Kansas, as an edible legume for growing with perennial grains in a non-tillage permaculture system. Reports say that it can self-sow to the point of nuisance and that its seed is rather bland. Both these points are positive, since it means that it crops well and that it can be easily flavoured with herbs etc for use as the protein part of a meal. Give the plant a sunny position in a well-drained soil.

Medicago sativa

Alfalfa grows very well in temperate regions so long as the appropriate rhizobium bacteria is present in the soil. This bacteria lives on the roots in a symbiotic relationship with the alfalfa and converts atmospheric nitrogen into a form that alfalfa can utilize, thus improving the growth of the plant. Alfalfa seeds are small and fiddly, but are often used for sprouting, making a very nutritious food. The seed can also be ground into flour and is mixed with wheat to make protein-rich bread. The young shoots can also be eaten raw or cooked. A drying oil from the seed is used in making paints etc. The plant is very deep rooted and makes an excellent long-term green manure.

Castanea sativa SWEET CHESTNUT

Juglans regia WALNUT

Glyceria spp MANNA GRASS

Medicago sativa ALFALFA

Quercus ilex HOLM OAK

Torreya nucifera

Triticum aestivum WHEAT

Beckmannia eruciformis

Caragana species

Cephalotaxus harringtonii

Desmanthus illinoensis

42 Plants For A Future: *www.pfaf.org*

Vegetable Oils

Many species of plants produce seeds containing fats - these fats are used as a food reserve for the developing seedling and they are quite often present in sufficient quantities to make their extraction, in the form of oil, worthwhile. Vegetable oil has a wide range of uses, and whilst many of these involve processes that are too technical for small-scale ventures, there are still many ways in which we can employ them - as a food for example, or as a lubricant, a fuel for paraffin lamps and as a wood preservative.

Oils are often divided into three categories according to their qualities, these categories are non-drying, semi- drying and drying. Non-drying oils are slow to oxidise and so remain liquid for a long time. This quality makes them particularly useful as lubricants and as a fuel for lamps. Drying oils, on the other hand, are quite quick to oxidise and become solid, thus they are often used in paints and varnishes -Linseed oil is a good example of this. Semi-drying oils have qualities intermediate between the above two groups.

Almost all commercially grown oil seed crops in the temperate zone are of annual plants. The list is quite long and it is not intended to deal with them in this section but some of the most common ones are Rape, Soya, Linseed, Sunflower and Safflower. There are also, however, quite a few perennial species that could be utilised for oil production and some of the more promising of these are described below. Unless stated otherwise they all produce an edible oil.

Althaea officinalis

The Marshmallow is a herbaceous plant native to Britain and growing wild on the upper margins of brackish marshes, along ditches and banks, often near the sea. As the common name suggests, the roasted root of the plant was used as a confection long before the sweet of that name was made. This plant is easily cultivated, growing well in most soils and tolerant of fairly dry conditions. The seed is produced quite freely, but it is quite small and tedious to harvest by hand. The oil is drying. Other uses for this plant include edible leaves, raw or cooked, glue made from the root, an egg-white substitute that can be made from water in which the plant has been cooked, and stem and root fibres in paper making.

Camellia species

Evergreen shrubs from China and Japan. This group includes the well-known garden Camellias. They are quite hardy but dislike cold winds and alkaline soils, probably growing best in thin woodland. They are sometimes cultivated as an oil crop in the Orient, this oil is non-drying and is especially popular as a hair dressing. Species to try are japonica (the garden Camellia), C. olifera and C. sasanqua.

Cephalotaxus harringtonia

Is an evergreen coniferous shrub from the woodlands of Japan. It grows in most soils, succeeds in heavy shade but prefers light shade and dislikes exposed positions. Plants are either male or female but have been known to change sex. Obviously both sexes should be grown if seed is wanted (one male for every five females) although there are reports of isolated females producing fruits with infertile seed. Both seed and fruit are edible but can taste resinous.

Cornus sanguinea

The Dogwood, is a native deciduous shrub found wild in mixed woods, scrub and hedgerows on calcareous soils, though it succeeds on most soils. It can also be grown as a hedge. The oil, which is non- drying, is obtained from both the seed and pericarp (the fleshy shell surrounding the seed). It is said to be edible when refined. Young branches of the plant are used in basket making and a grey-blue dye is obtained from the fruit.

Corylus avellana

The British native Hazel, is a deciduous shrub of woods and hedgerows found especially on calcareous soils but succeeding on most soils. The oil is non-drying. As well as its seed, Hazel was once widely grown in coppices to provide wood for making hurdles, wattles, fences, etc. It might also be worthwhile trying other members of this genus such as C. colurna, and C. sieboldiana mandschurica (synonym C. mandschurica).

Fagus sylvatica

The British native Beech tree grows on most soils but avoids heavy, wet ones, it is abundant on chalk. Heavy crops are not produced every year. The oil is semi-drying and is said to store for a long time without growing rancid. The seed is also edible as are the young leaves that are produced in the two flushes of growth in spring and mid-summer.

Glaucium flavum

The Horned Poppy is another British native species found on shingle banks of the coast. It is easily grown in any good garden soil but is, unfortunately, a fairly short-lived perennial. The oil is said to burn very cleanly in lamps.

Edible Plants

Juglans regia

The Walnut tree, is more or less naturalised in southern England. It succeeds on most soils, preferring a deep loam, and strongly disliking windy positions. The oil is drying and quickly goes rancid. The seed is, of course, edible and amongst its other uses, the crushed leaves can be used as an insect repellent. Other Juglans species also have oil rich seeds although they may not be produced freely in temperate regions. It might be worthwhile trying J. cinerea, J .mandschurica or J nigra.

Prunus species

This genus includes the Plum, Cherry, Almond, Apricot and Peach. The seed of all members of this genus could probably by used for oil extraction, although in our climate the Plum is probably the most reliable choice. The oil is semi-drying. One word of warning though, if the extracted oil should taste strongly of bitter almonds then it should only be consumed in small quantities.

Rhus verniciflua (Toxicodendron vernicifluum)

The Japanese Lacquer tree is a deciduous tree from the woodlands of China and Japan. It succeeds in ordinary garden soil but is susceptible to Coral Spot fungus. The oil is drying. Indeed it is actually solid at room temperature and so can be used as a vegetable tallow in making candles. All parts of this tree including the oil are poisonous. A natural varnish or lacquer can be obtained from the sap of the tree.

Vitis vinifera

This is the Grape. Due to the size of the seed it would not normally be practicable to cultivate for oil production but if you grow a reasonable quality of grapes for wine or have access to someone else s pulp from winemaking, then you could have a go. The oil is edible when refined and is also used in lighting.

Finally, a few words on extracting the oil. The best method to use if the oil is to be eaten is to squeeze out the oil in a press. As far as we know, there are no sources of domestic size oil presses in Britain, perhaps a fruit press could be adapted. Prior to crushing, it will improve extraction rates if you grind up the seed somewhat. This method of extraction will not get all the oil out however. If you then boil up the pulp, a lot more oil will then float to the surface of the water and be skimmed off. This oil is not so wholesome to use as a food but is perfectly alright for all its other applications. The oil should be stored in airtight containers.

Althaea officinalis MARSHMALLOW

Camellia species

Corylus avellana HAZEL

Vitis vinifera GRAPE

Glaucium flavum HORNED POPPY

Fagus sylvatica BEECH

Prunus species

Prunus species

Rhus verniciflua LACQUER TREE

Edible Plants **45**

Fruit - Food of the Gods

What is a Fruit?

Many plants produce fruits in order to help in the dispersal of their seeds. It would be pointless for a plant to drop all its seeds directly beneath, by its roots, since all the seedlings would then compete with each other and their parent. Plants have therefore evolved various mechanisms by which their seeds can be dispersed. Some plants, such as sycamore, have dry spiky or leathery fruits which may be dispersed by the wind, others such as burdock have barbs that attach themselves to animals fur or our clothing, but the fruits that we are interested in here are those fleshy fruits which the plant has made attractive for animals to eat.

As the seeds mature, the ovary and sometimes also the receptacle swell up around the seeds to become a juicy, fleshy and often sweet fruit. The seeds inside usually have a tough outer coat so that when the animal eats the fruit it will either, if the seeds are small, deposit the seeds unharmed in its faeces some distance from the parent plant e.g. the pips in soft fruit, or if the seed is large, as in plums, the fruit may be carried away and the seed dropped somewhere. Normally the fruit tastes awful before the seeds are ripe, so it will not get eaten before the seeds are mature enough to germinate. Seeds and fruit therefore ripen at the same time to ensure that the seeds are at the right stage when taken by an animal. Either way the animal has p aid for its nice meal by doing the plant a favour in dispersing it seeds.

One of the wonderful things about fruits is that we are actually eating something offered to us by the plant. Assuming that we are living a fairly natural lifestyle -i.e. not eating imported fruit that could never grow in this climate, eating fresh fruit that is in season, not eating seedless varieties, not throwing fruit seeds or cores into the rubbish bin where they have no chance of re-entering the natural cycle - then you could say that the plant would want us to eat the fruit. In turn the plant has done us a favour by producing this nice juicy, tasty morsel full of naturally filtered water, natural sugars, flavours, vitamins and minerals and other nutrients. Fruits are amongst the most delicious foods on Earth. Most are light and easy to digest and they are a natural convenience food because there is normally no preparation needed.

The Nutritional Value of Fruits

Most fruits are very easy to digest because food is stored in the fruit as sugars. (Unripe fruits are often high in starch and organic acids, which makes them taste very sour, and these are converted to sugars only as the fruit ripens). Most fruits contain no fats at all though some, such as olives and avocados have quite a high fat content. Whilst it is not really feasible to grow these fruits in temperate areas, we can grow Elaeagnus and Hippophae berries which contain Essential Fatty Acids (EFA s).

Most fruits also contain no protein. Protein and fats are present in the seed but this is usually not eaten (e.g. in plums) or passes straight through (pips in berries) so fruits are NOT a complete food and could not really be recommended as the sole part of the diet. Also, unless you eat Special Berries (see below) all year round, you will go quite short of minerals. Most fruits are particularly low in calcium and magnesium which are necessary for healthy teeth and bones.

Fruits are also very low in zinc which is essential for the function of the immune system, the formation of skin, the healing of wounds, brain function and it is essential for the function of the reproductive organs. But do not despair, this deficiency can be made up by eating plenty of green leaves (see the section Green Gold).

Fruits are best eaten fresh, ripe and raw. There is normally no need to cook them - unless you have a glut and want to preserve some by bottling it (which can be done without sugar if your jar has a good seal), or if there are windfall apples that are not ripe enough to eat raw. But it is preferable if cooked fruit only forms a small part of the diet, as it is so much healthier and more satisfying to eat them raw.

A word of warning about fruits for those who are not use to eating much of it: Like leaves, fruits are a very strongly cleansing food, capable of stirring up and removing toxins that were long buried in the body. (These toxins come from certain foods, especially j unk food with chemical additives, an excess of meat, dairy products etc. and environmental toxins). However unlike leaves, which actually help to carry toxins out of the body as well, fruits often tend to stir them up without carrying them away. So if you know that your diet has not been all it could have been over the last few years and that your system is liable to be rather toxic, then please approach fruit with caution.

Do not suddenly eat a lot of fruit in one go (especially of the more acid berries) until you know that your system can cope with it. What is liable to happen is that a lot of toxins will be stirred up into what is known as a Healing Crisis and you will feel ill. Perhaps you will blame the healthy diet for making you ill and perhaps even go to the doctor for some pills. These will only suppress the symptoms and drive the toxins deeper into the body, as well as adding more toxins, -so you will be worse off than before. So unless you understand about healing crises and know how to manage them, please go easy on the fruit if you are not used to it. Many Naturopaths have used short-term fruit diets for healing with a great deal of success. This is because of the wonderful cleansing and healing properties of fruits, especially if accompanied by green leaves or leaf juices. However this tends to be too drastic for most people nowadays because of the general decrease in health and nutrition of the overall population. This is still possible to do but we would only recommend it under the guidance of a qualified Naturopath or Nutritional Therapist.

The types of fruit

Fruits contain quite good levels of vitamins but are quite low in many important minerals. On their own, they will not provide you with enough minerals. Indeed, if you just ate fruit and nothing else for a while, you might lose all your teeth. So perhaps it would be all right to eat a lot of fruit as long as one eats a lot of leaves as well? If you study the tables of mineral composition of various different fruits, three main groups emerge.

1) The large cultivated fruits such as apples, pears and tomatoes.

Although these form the bulk of most people s fruit intake, they are pretty low in minerals and vitamins. They have been selectively bred, sometimes over thousands of years, in order to produce a bigger size, milder flavour, more sugar and higher water content. Unfortunately the nutrient content has sadly lost out. Hence the wild crab apples and pears - though often inedible due to their acidity and astringency - are actually more nutritious than the cultivated ones. A clear example of this can be seen if we look at the tomato. The wild tomato is no larger than a cherry, yet a single fruit contains more vitamins and minerals than a single much larger cultivated tomato. When comparing the size of each fruit you begin to realise just how much nutrient we have lost from many of our cultivated foods!

2). Small berries such as strawberries, raspberries, blackberries, blackcurrants and gooseberries.

These are far richer in minerals than the first group. Although these berries have also been bred up for size etc., they are much closer to their natural state than the big fruits, and consequently are richer in nutrients. However, they still do not compare in nutritional value to green leaves vThe berries are also higher in fibre (the pips really do help to keep you regular!) and lower in calories.

3). The special berries.

These are normally wild plants that have not been bred up and hence not been devitalised and demineralised in that way. They are much richer in nutrients than the other fruits and also often have great medicinal value. A few examples are mentioned below: -.

• Hippophae and Elaeagnus These, and especially the Hippophae, are the special fruits par excellence. They are probably the most nutritious fruits you can grow in the Temperate zone and are a very rich source of vitamins and minerals. In particular they are very good sources of vitamin C and bioflavinoids, as well as containing essential fatty acids (EFA's). (See the pfaf.org website on Hippophae salicifolia and Elaeagnus x ebbingei for more details.)

• Rosehips. Whilst wild rosehips are extremely nutritious, most are small and fiddly to harvest and use because the layer of flesh covering the hairy seeds is very thin. However, Rosa rugosa has particularly large hips which can be eaten much more easily (and certain varieties have larger fruits than others). Another good source of vitamin C, it also contains some EFA s and is also very high in carotene or provitamin A, the precursor of vitamin A. While true vitamin A or retinol, which is only found in animal products, is toxic in large amounts, carotene is found in plant foods and is totally non-toxic. The body only makes as much vitamin A from it as it needs. Ripe Rosa rugosa fruits are also extremely delicious - true ambrosia!

Edible Plants **47**

• Hawthorns. Whilst the fruits of the British two native hawthorns are edible few people are going to want to eat many of them. However, there are several species with cherry-size fruits that are absolutely delicious to eat. Again these fruits are high in bioflavonoids and fairly high in vitamin C. They also have several useful medicinal properties including making a good heart tonic whilst reducing high blood pressure and cholesterol levels in the blood. See the pfaf.org website on hawthorns for more information.

• Barberries (Berberis). These fruits usually have a rather acid flavour, but are pleasant nonetheless and go very well in muesli. They have a particularly beneficial effect on the urinary system, that they cleanse and stimulate.

It is particularly important that we take in vitamin C because so much of our food is cooked nowadays and thus largely devoid of vitamin C. Also, during evolution we lost the ability to manufacture Vitamin C in our own bodies so we are at a disadvantage to most other animals that can. This is one of the reasons why we need to eat lots of fresh raw food. Vitamin C is also useful in the treatment of many diseases ranging from colds to cancer.

Elaeagnus and Hippophae are very rich in bioflavonoids, which are beneficial plant pigments that assist in the utilisation of vitamin C and are said to improve the function of the brain. Bioflavonoids are also very beneficial to our health in many other ways. For example, the bioflavonoids found in the fruits of all Elaeagnus and Hippophae species have been shown to be an effective preventative for and treatment of cancer.

EFA s are essential for the formation of healthy cell membranes and necessary for many body functions especially that of the immune system. Hence these fruits are extremely beneficial, but are of particular benefit for those with diseases of the immune system such as MS, ME, rheumatoid arthritis, juvenile onset diabetes, cancer and AIDS. This is especially true of the Hippophae. Considering also that high levels of vitamin C, B vitamins and minerals are also beneficial to the immune system, these berries are a particularly good food, tonic and medicine for anyone with an under functioning immune system.

So the general conclusion is that all fruit is good for you but some are more nutritious than others. They are not as nutritious as leaves, but they do taste better because the plant has deliberately laced the fruit with sugars and pleasant flavours to tempt us.

The fresh fruit season

It is important, as far as possible, to eat fruit that is fresh, ripe and in season. Fruits that are picked unripe will never

develop their full flavour, sweetness or nutritional value because the plant hasn t had enough time to put all it wanted to in the fruit. Fruit that has been transported halfway across the globe is normally picked under ripe and sprayed to stop it rotting. It is also not in harmony with the climatic zone in which we live so is much less good for us, as well as contributing to unnecessary pollution in the transportation process. The ideal way to eat fruit is to eat it straight from the plant. Once it starts to age it loses its nutritional value in the same way as other parts of the plant do.

With careful planning it is possible to pick fresh fruit from your garden for 10 or even eleven months of the year. The season starts with the evergreen Elaeagnus in early April. These will continue to crop until the middle or end of May when Mahonias and the first strawberries ripen. The variety of fruits then increases considerably with the greatest abundance coming in late summer and early autumn. There are, however, many different fruits that can be harvested in late autumn and early winter. These include the Hippophae, which can be harvested until the middle of January, and various Gaultherias, which can be picked in early spring. However, these late harvests are usually quite small in quantity - more a nibble than a real meal.

Fruits that store

In order to extend the season, there are certain fruits that store very well with little loss of nutrient. Thus you can ensure a supply of fresh fruit throughout the winter, spring and early summer when few or no berries are available.

• The apple is the best example for this climate. There are many late-ripening varieties that will keep for varying amounts of time in storage, the latest storing for a whole year or more in good condition. These late keeping apples are normally not actually ready to be eaten when they are harvested. When in storage, the starches and acids in the fruit are gradually converted to sugars and the fruit becomes ripe over a period of weeks or months. If the late apples were allowed to ripen fully on the tree they would get damaged by the weather and eaten by the birds before they ripened properly, so they would not store at all. While not the most nutritious fruit, they are very good for ensuring a year round supply of fresh fruit in this climate.

• Certain pear varieties will keep for several months in a similar way to apples though each variety ripens over a much shorter period so you can end up with a sudden glut of fruit that will quickly go over-ripe and then rot if they are not eaten in time.

• Contrary to popular opinion, kiwi fruits can be grown very successfully in many temperate areas including Britain. If the fruits are picked in early winter, they will keep in a cool store for several months. Kiwis are actually very nutritious, being very high in vitamin C and also good sources of carotene and folic acid (because of their green colour).

• There are stories of the Victorians storing grapes in cellars over winter. Grapes can be grown in temperate climates but most varieties tend to be small and sour unless grown in a green house because our summers are not hot enough to ripen the fruit. Try growing varieties such as Brandt or Isabella which do much better here. Also, select your growing position carefully - a south or west facing wall should give best results. In terms of nutritional value grapes can probably be classified with the berries. They have a moderate amount of folic acid due to their light green colour. (Purple grapes also have some green in them.)

• Golden berries are closely related to tomatoes, but have a much richer flavour. Any green fruits left on the plant when the first frosts come along can be stored in a cool place and will ripen slowly over the next few months.

• The bletted fruits. Certain fruits, such as Mespilus germanica (the medlar) and Sorbus domestica, (the service tree) do not ripen fully in temperate climates. They are picked in late autumn and will then ripen slowly in store. They do not become edible raw until they are almost at the point of going rotten (a process known as bletting), but when at this stage taste like a delicious tropical fruit. However, you do need to be careful because if you overdo the bletting the fruits will ferment in your stomach and cause digestive problems.

Therefore with the summer and autumn berries, and stored apples (and possibly pears and kiwis) over the winter and spring, it is very possible to be totally self sufficient in fruit in this climate.

In Conclusion

• Fruits are amongst the most delectable and delicious foods on Earth, and unlike other foods, are actually deliberately produced by the plant to be eaten. This is not pure altruism on their behalf, but symbiosis or co-operation, because in return they want their seeds to be dispersed. They are also the ideal healthy convenience or snack food because you can just pick them up and eat them - no preparation is usually needed - just make sure they are ripe.

• Most conventional shop bought fruit is a reasonable source of vitamins, depending on how fresh it is, but is not very rich in minerals. The ideal suppliers of vitamins and minerals are the green leaves (See Green Gold section).

• The small wild and semi wild berries are far more nutrient-rich because they are closer to their natural state and have not had the nutrients bred out of them. Some berries such as Elaeagnus, Hippophae, Rosa Rugosa and Crataegus are particularly nutrient-rich and have numerous beneficial health giving properties. It is a good idea to include more berries in your diet, especially the Special Berries. The easiest and best way to do this is to grow them yourself because this ensures their availability, freshness and enables you to pick them at their best (assuming the birds don't get there first!)

(See the section on alternative fruits for more details).

• While being a very enjoyable and healthy food, please bear in mind that fruits are far from being a complete food, so do not rely on them too heavily - or your teeth might fall out! (this is particularly true of the imbalanced commercial fruit).

• In most fruits food is stored in the form of sugars so they are a very light and easy to digest food. Digestive problems will respond quite well to a temporary diet of fruit to give it a rest from heavy foods.

• A few fruits do contain fats, but most have none or virtually no protein. This is stored in their seeds.

• Fruits are very cleansing and detoxifying and in this way are very helpful in the treatment of diseases. If you have a cold, flu or other infection, a fruit (and leaf) diet will clear it out of you faster. They are also very helpful in the treatment of chronic diseases. But unless you are absolutely sure of what you are doing, and can cope with the possibility of a flare up (Healing Crisis) without going to the doctor for suppressive drugs, then using fruit for healing purposes must be done under the supervision of a qualified practitioner.

Green Gold - The Leaves of Life!

The Importance of Green Leaves to the Planet

The chlorophyll in green leaves forms the basis for all life on Earth. Without it life as we know it would not exist. There might be a few chemosynthetic bacteria left, since these can obtain energy from chemical reactions other than photosynthesis, but that would be it. Virtually all life depends on that beautiful green chlorophyll molecule.

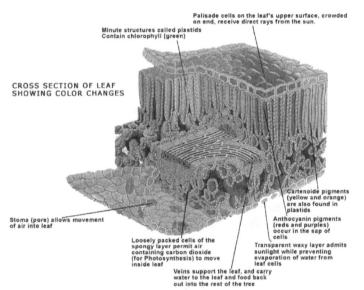

The chlorophyll pigment is concentrated in the leaves of plants -though it is also present in other parts such as the stems of many herbaceous plants, flower buds and certain fruits and occasionally roots. The chlorophyll molecule is responsible for trapping the sun's energy; and this solar energy is converted to chemical energy in the form of glucose using carbon dioxide (CO_2) from the atmosphere, and water (H_2O) from the soil. This glucose is then transported all round the plant for use as required. Some is oxidised for energy, some is stored as insoluble starch when it is not required immediately. Some is converted into cellulose to make new plant structures e.g. more leaves, stems, flowers, roots. Some is taken to fruits and accumulated there. Some is used to make proteins utilising nitrogen from the soil.

All plants live and grow by photosynthesis. The only exceptions to this are extreme parasites such as dodder (which have lost their chlorophyll) and saprophytes such as the ghost orchid, most fungi and bacteria. The saprophytes feed off dead and decaying vegetation, whilst the parasites feed off living plants and so both are dependent on green plants and chlorophyll, even though they do not possess it.

Green plants are the primary producers as a result of their wonderful greenness! Many animals -including humans -eat plants. Some animals eat other animals, but if you follow the food chain back you will find that green plants are always at the base. Animals and plants die and decay, releasing minerals into the soil and CO_2 into the air for green plants to use for photosynthesis. Thus the cycle continues, and we all (except a few bacteria) need green plants. If green plants were to suddenly disappear, then so would virtually all life on Earth - including Homo Sapiens.

Green leaves are thus the powerhouses -the great driving force for Life on Earth. Photosynthesis is the life generating chemical process. Chlorophyll is thus the Molecule of Life.

The Importance of Green Leaves to Health.

It is no small wonder then that green leaves are so very extremely beneficial to the health.

1. Vital Life Energy. When you eat a leaf you are taking into your body -into your very being -that wonderful source of energy and vitality that powers life on Earth. It is no coincidence that the haemoglobin molecule (which is responsible for carrying oxygen in our blood and distributing it to all our cells, as well as picking up CO_2 and taking it back to the lungs for excretion) is very similar in structure to that of chlorophyll. The main difference is that haemoglobin contains iron whilst chlorophyll contains magnesium. Some people even believe that by eating chlorophyll you actually make haemoglobin directly!

Freshly picked raw leaves in particular are teeming with activity and vitality. Kirlian photography can measure this vitality, or life force, and it reduces when an individual plant or animal becomes sick or very old. When you eat fresh raw leaves you are taking that vitality into you. Leaves that have been picked and stored for a while, or leaves which have been cooked or dried will have much less vitality, but will still be very beneficial. Eat Green Leaves - take in LIFE!

The chlorophyll molecule itself is very soothing and healing and is useful in healing wounds. It is also a wonderful de¬odouriser and can help to remove unpleasant smells from the gut!

2. Vitamins and Minerals. When first changing from an animal based to a plant based diet, people often wonder where they will obtain their minerals, vitamins, protein and fats. All these questions will be answered in this section. Green leaves can provide most of the nutrients that we require.

Of all the many foods, green leaves are actually the richest in vitamins and minerals. The reason for this is that these nutrients are also required in photosynthesis -hence our heavy emphasis in this book on plants with edible leaves.

Green leaves are the foods richest in easily utilised calcium. On a dry weight basis, chemical analysis shows that most plant leaves are actually as rich, or richer, in calcium than cow s milk. This may come as a surprise to most people -but the figures are official! Cow's (or goat's) milk is in fact

not a very good source of calcium at all because milk is very mucus -forming and tends to generate large amounts of sticky mucus in the gut. This mucus interferes with digestion and absorption, so the calcium it contains is not well utilised. In addition to this, calcium requires magnesium for its utilisation in the body - without sufficient magnesium, calcium cannot be utilised properly. Milk is a poor source of magnesium, while green leaves, are a rich source of both calcium and magnesium together. Also, unlike milk, green leaves are very clean, light foods that the body finds easy to handle, and they actually help to clear the body of mucous and toxins. It is very interesting to note that the incidence of osteoporosis is very high in the so called developed countries where large amounts of milk and meat are consumed; but is much lower in countries where few animal products are eaten.

Incidentally, when we talk about green leaves, we mean leaves that are green, not the pale white hearts found inside cabbage, lettuce, celery or chicory hearts - or any other blanched vegetable. The dark green leaves with beneficial properties are those found on plants of dandelion, green chicory, parsley, kale, various campanulas, thyme, reichardia, violas etc. See our sections on Winter Salads, Edible Leaves etc. for more examples.

Green leaves are also extremely rich sources of potassium - a mineral that tends to be lacking in the processed diet of industrial society. The potassium and sodium are in balance, there being much more potassium than sodium -which is the natural order of things. Processing foods tends to leach out the mineral rich and potassium rich part, and piles on lots of sodium in the form of salt, sodium bicarbonate (= bicarbonate of soda) and various other sodium salts. This excess of sodium causes serious imbalance in the body resulting in numerous health problems.

Green leaves are a very rich source of iron. They are also good sources of zinc, manganese cobalt, copper and many other minerals that we need, but tend not to think much about. They are also a rich source of the whole B complex (except perhaps B12 -which can be obtained by other means -see later). Pregnant women are often advised to take vitamin supplements, and especially folic acid, in order to prevent Spina bifida in babies. All they have to do, of course, is make sure they eat a salad every day since, of course, foliage is the best source of folic acid. The B complex is involved in many

different bodily functions, but two of the most important ones are:-

1. The release of energy from food.

2. Maintaining the immune system.

So if you keep feeling tired or keep catching colds, perhaps you need to eat more green leaves!

Green leaves are the richest sources of carotene, or provitamin A, from which the body easily makes as much vitamin A as it needs. Pure vitamin A or retinol (found in animal products) is highly toxic if eaten to excess -Arctic explorers have been known to die from vitamin A and vitamin D poisoning after eating the livers of polar bears since this is where these vitamins are stored in particularly high concentration. Carotene is totally non toxic and in fact is very beneficial and healing in large quantities. It is a very useful antioxidant vitamin in these days of high pollution. There are reports of children going blind in India because they did not have enough vitamin A in their diet, which could have been prevented if they had regularly eaten green leaves, which would not have been expensive.

Carotene is also found in orange or yellow fruits or vegetables such as apricots and rosehips.

Freshly picked raw green leaves are excellent sources of vitamin C. Cooking, wilting, drying or storing the picked leaves in a warm place destroys much or all of the vitamin C, depending on how it is done. Amongst other things, vitamin C is very important for the function of the immune system, tissue repair, and it is an antioxidant vitamin. Vitamin C is present in all living and actively metabolising parts of plants, not just leaves (i.e. it is not present in dormant seeds, but is made in large amounts when seeds germinate.) Most people tend to be rather short of vitamin C because they do not eat enough fresh raw foods. Our forest dwelling ancestors living largely on fruits and leaves would have had an abundant supply of vitamin C.

We do not obtain vitamin D from leaves, but we can make our own if we regularly expose our skin to some sunlight. We do not need large quantities of sun for this, nor do we need to sunbathe all day, which would in any case risk skin damage or even cancer. We can also store vitamin D in the liver, so in effect we can stock up in the summer for the winter.

Vitamin E (another antioxidant vitamin) and vitamin K (essential for blood clotting) are also abundant in green leaves.

Bioflavonoids, which are sometimes known as 'vitamin F', are various plant pigments that occur in green leaves in association with the chlorophyll; and also in many fruits, especially small berries such as rosehips. They are important

Edible Plants **51**

for the utilisation of vitamin C and some people believe they are very good for the brain. Bioflavonoids are beneficial to our health in many other ways. Thus rutin, which is found in the leaves of buckwheat, is a bioflavonoid that has a very beneficial effect on the circulatory system. The bioflavonoids found in the fruits of all Eleagnus and Hippophae species have been shown to be an effective preventative for and treatment of cancer.

3. Essential Fatty Acids Although leaves are very low in fats, the small amounts of fat that they do contain tend to consist of the essential fatty acids linoleic and alpha-linoleic acid. These are essential for the health of the immune system and in making cell membranes.

4. Proteins Believe it or not, green leaves contain a fair amount of top quality protein. On a dry weight basis, leaves are about 25% protein, comparable to beans. And unlike the storage proteins of most seeds, which tend to be somewhat short of one or more essential amino acid, green leaves are high in all of these substances. The reason for this is that leaf protein is actually in the form of enzymes (biological catalysts which speed up and direct biochemical reactions such as those responsible for photosynthesis, respiration, digestion, and so on.) These are the many enzymes that work with that wonderful chlorophyll molecule in the process of photosynthesis. Of course no-one would recommend that you use leaves as your sole source of protein, but the protein content is present and not to be sneezed at.

As well as providing protein, the enzymes in raw leaves, and in other raw plant foods, actually help in the digestion of the particular food in which they are found, and are very beneficial to the body.

There is an association called L eaf for Life / Find your Feet which juices leaves and uses this as a protein supplement for children in countries like India. The resulting product is called L eafu and has greatly improved the health of many people there. The other advantage of leaf protein is that it is soluble and therefore easily digestible -unlike many other forms of protein. .

5. Fibre Leaves are an excellent source of healthy fibre. Lack of fibre (usually due to a diet of processed foods and animal products) causes pain, constipation and disease. Adequate fibre results in regular soft stools and health. The fibre in leaves is particularly beneficial and much healthier than excessive amounts of bran (from wheat) that can act as an intestinal irritant. In fact the fibre present in fresh raw leaves encourages the f riendly lactobacteria - mainly Lactobacillus acidophilus in the intestines to proliferate and grow there. These bacteria thrive on green stuff. Inside us they make B vitamins (including B12) and vitamin K. They

help in the digestion of food, help our immune system and help in keeping the u nfriendly bacteria at bay. The u nfriendly putrefactive bacteria, such as E.coli, proliferate when there is an absence of fibre and an abundance of decomposing remains of meat and milk. They do not make any vitamins, and instead encourage the putrefaction (rather than digestion) of food and produce toxins and foul smells in the process. These bowel toxins are a major cause of disease in western society - and can even result in colon cancer. It is often said that disease starts in a toxic colon. So - eat plenty of raw leaves to encourage the friendly lactobacteria.

6. Medicines In addition to using green leaves as a food, specific green leaves make excellent natural medicines. Leaves generally are very cleansing, healing, soothing and revitalising as well as being very nourishing. A green leaf juice is in fact an excellent nutritional supplement, and such juices are often used in natural therapies, including in the treatment of cancer. As Hippocrates the Father of Medicine said "Let Food be Your Medicine and Medicine be your Food". Specific leaves are good for specific things. For example dandelions and chicory are good for the liver and kidneys and are good blood purifiers. Dandelions are also good diuretics, but, unlike diuretic drugs which deplete the body of minerals, especially potassium, dandelions are so high in potassium and other minerals that the body has a considerable positive gain in potassium despite the diuretic effect.

Nettles (and of course we don t recommend you eat these raw) are good blood purifiers and help in the treatment of arthritis.

Mint and fennel leaves contain aromatic oils which help with the digestion of food and also dispel intestinal gases. The juice from comfrey leaves and or Aloe Vera leaves applied directly to a wound, burn or ulcer, will greatly speed up the healing process.

(If you want more information on this aspect of leaves then see 'The New Holistic Herbal' by David Hoffman, 'The Dictionary of Modern Herbalism' by Simon Mills and 'The RHS Encyclopaedia of Herbs and their Uses' by Deni Bown.

To summarize

It It is the chlorophyll in green leaves that is responsible for virtually all life on earth. Leaves are the powerhouses of plants, where sunlight energy is transformed into plant energy. And when we eat leaves we take in this energy, and vitality. Green leaves have some unique properties and most people would benefit from making an effort to grow or seek out more of them for inclusion in their diet.

Useful Weeds

When Ken and Addy Fern were actively working on their experimental plot in Cornwall, visitors would have noticed the large amount of weeds that grew there. This was partly because they simply didn t have enough time to keep on top of all the weeds, but also because many are quite useful, and some were even actively encouraged. Their approach was that a weed is merely a plant growing somewhere they didn t want it to grow and, instead of automatically hoeing out any plant that didn t put there, try and leave in all those that are not likely to interfere with the other plants they were growing.

There are several ways in which weeds can be helpful to leave in the garden. Many of them, for example, are edible (indeed some are very tasty), whilst others have medicinal properties or other uses. Weeds also help to provide a more balanced environment by providing food and habitats for insects and other creatures - this can have a very important knock-on effect for the gardener by encouraging beneficial insects and birds and thus reducing insect predation on our plants. In addition, weeds help to protect and feed the soil by providing good compost material as well as by covering it and preventing erosion.

Whilst, with a few notable exceptions, we would not recommend deliberately introducing weeds into the garden, it is quite possible to co-exist happily with many of them, particularly many of the annual species such as bittercress, chickweed and shepherd s purse. It is simply a matter of making sure you weed out most of the seedlings, leaving a few to grow on and then allowing them to set seed. There are, however, some perennials, such as couch grass and Japanese knotweed, which are so vigorous that they really cannot be tolerated in amongst your prize plants -they will simply swamp them.

The following list includes some of the weeds that can be particularly useful, though not all plants listed should be tolerated due to their aggressive tendencies.

Aegopodium podagraria

Ground Elder is a vigorous and very invasive perennial, growing about 60cm tall and spreading rapidly by its roots. It is very difficult to eradicate because any small piece of root left in the ground will quickly regrow. Whilst it is occasionally grown as a ground cover in the wilder parts of the garden (shrubs and strong growing bulbs such as some lilies grow very well through it), it really is too vigorous for most other herbaceous species. There is, however, a variegated form of this species that is less invasive and is sometimes grown in the ornamental garden. Ground Elder has a long history of edible and medicinal use; indeed it was cultivated as a food crop and medicinal herb in the Middle Ages. It was used mainly as a food that could counteract gout, one of the effects of the rich foods eaten by monks, bishops etc at this time. The leaves can be eaten raw or cooked and have an unusual tangy flavour which is an acquired taste, although some people like it.

Allium vineale

Crow Garlic is a perennial bulb that grows up to 60cm tall. As a weed, it is most likely to be found in lawns that are not cut very regularly and spreads by means of the small bulbils that it produces instead of flowers. Both the bulbs and the bulbils have a rather strong garlic-like flavour -the bulbs can be harvested virtually all year round whilst the bulbils are ready in the summer. The leaves are also edible, with a similar flavour, but tend to have a stringy texture.

Capsella bursa-pastoris

Shepherd s Purse is an annual plant growing up to 50cm tall in rich soils, but much smaller in poor ones. A very common garden weed, it can flower and produce seeds all year round and will often spread freely in cultivated ground. This species is a prime example of how a plant can be viewed as an annoying weed in some areas of the world, whilst in others it is actually cultivated for its wide range of uses. It is extensively cultivated in some areas of the world as a cabbage-flavoured spring greens, whilst in Japan it is one of the essential ingredients of a ceremonial rice and barley gruel that is eaten on January 7th. The leaves grow rather larger under cultivation, they can be harvested about a month after sowing and can be treated as a cut and come again crop. The young leaves, used before the plant comes into flower, make a fine addition to salads, whilst older leaves are a cress and cabbage substitute, becoming peppery with age. The young flowering shoots can be eaten in the same way as broccoli. They are rather thin and fiddly but the taste is quite acceptable. The seed is rich in oil and, although small and very fiddly to harvest, can be eaten raw or cooked - it used to be ground into a meal and used in soups etc. The seedpods can be used as a peppery seasoning for soups and stews, whilst the fresh or dried root is used as a ginger substitute. The plant has long been used as a domestic herbal remedy, particularly in the treatment of both internal and external bleeding, diarrhoea etc. The seed, when placed in water, attracts mosquitoes. It has a gummy substance that binds the insects mouth to the seed. The seed also releases a substance toxic to the larvae - a kilo of seed is said to be able to kill 10 million larvae.

Cardamine species

Bittercress is a very common annual garden weed, growing just 1cm tall in very poor soils but up to 30cm in richer

Edible Plants **53**

conditions. It spreads very freely by means of its seeds but is easily controlled by hoeing. It also tends to like growing in pots and it can be time consuming having to weed pot plants by hand. There are two main species found in gardens, the hairy bittercress C. hirsuta, and wavy bittercress C. flexuosa. Bittercress can be in flower all year round, especially if the winter is mild. Both the leaves and flowers can be eaten, raw and cooked. They have a hot cress-like flavour and can be used as a garnish or flavouring in salads, though they can also be used as a potherb.

Chenopodium album

Fat Hen is another annual weed that used to be cultivated as a food plant. Growing about 80cm tall, it was at one time often grown for its edible leaves. There is still one named variety that can sometimes be obtained - called Magenta in reference to the colour of its leaves, it is considered by some people to be the best tasting of all potherbs. The leaves are a very acceptable spinach substitute, the taste is a little bland but this can be improved by adding a few stronger-flavoured leaves. The young flowering stems can also be eaten in much the same way as broccoli. The edible seed, which is somewhat fiddly to harvest, can be dried and ground into a meal and eaten raw or baked into bread. It can also be sprouted and added to salads. The seed should be soaked in water overnight and thoroughly rinsed before being used in order to remove any bitter-tasting saponins.

Cirsium species

There are many different species of thistle, the two you are most likely to encounter as weeds are C. arvense, the Creeping Thistle a perennial plant growing to about 90cm, and C. vulgare, the Common Thistle which is biennial and grows up to 2 metres tall. These are very aggressive weeds, the first spreading freely by means of its roots and the other sending its seeds far and wide to grow where you least expect them. The young roots of both species can be eaten raw or cooked. Although nutritious, they are rather bland with a taste reminiscent of Jerusalem artichokes. They are probably best when used in a mixture with other vegetables. Be warned though, just like Jerusalem artichokes the root is rich in inulin, a starch that cannot be digested by humans. This starch thus passes straight through the digestive system and, in some people, ferments to produce flatulence. The young stems can be peeled and cooked like asparagus or rhubarb. Young leaves have a fairly bland flavour and can also be eaten raw or cooked, but the prickles need to be removed before the leaves can be eaten - not only is this rather fiddly but very little edible leaf remains.

Elytrigia repens

Couch grass is one of the most pernicious weeds that gardeners have to contend with. It would be a very brave or very foolish person who would encourage this perennial grass into their garden. Growing about 50cm tall, the roots spread quickly through the soil, growing into the roots of other plants and making them almost impossible to get out. Even a small section of root left in the soil will quickly start growing again. Despite its antisocial tendency in the garden, however, couch is a very useful herbal medicine and the famous Herbalist Culpepper is said to have stated that half an acre of couch was worth five acres of carrots twice over. The edible uses of couch are very minor. The roots have been dried and ground into a powder, then used with wheat when making bread. Although thin and stringy, they contain starch and enzymes and are quite sweet. When boiled for a long time to break down the leathery membrane, syrup can be made from the roots and this is sometimes brewed into a beer. When roasted, the root has been ground into a powder and used as a healthier coffee substitute. Couch grass, however, is of considerable value as a herbal medicine -a decoction of the roots being very useful in the treatment of a wide range of kidney, liver and urinary disorders. They have a gentle remedial effect that is well tolerated by the body and has no side effects. This plant is also a favourite medicine of domestic cats and dogs, which will often eat quite large quantities of the leaves.

Epilobium angustifolium

With its tiny seed that floats so well on the air, rosebay willow herb will find its way to your garden without the need for you to invite it in. Left to its own devices, this perennial plant will then spread rapidly at the roots to form large clumps up to 2 metres tall. It produces spikes of flowers through much of the summer and, if it weren t so aggressive, it would surely merit a place in the ornamental garden.

The young leaves and shoot tips have been used in salads or cooked as a vegetable. When boiled they are said to make a wholesome vegetable and are a good source of vitamins A and C. The root can be eaten raw, cooked or dried and ground into a powder. When used in spring, it is said to have a sweet taste. The flower stalks, picked when the flowers are still in bud, can be eaten raw or cooked. The pith of young or older stems is slightly sweet, tender and quite pleasing to eat, though there is not much of it. A sweet and pleasant tea can be made from the dried leaves - it can be consumed on its own or mixed with conventional tea. Rosebay willow herb has often been used as a domestic herbal remedy, particularly to treat conditions such as diarrhoea and irritable bowel syndrome; it is used in Germany and Austria to treat prostate problems and a poultice of the leaves is applied to mouth ulcers. A poultice made from the peeled roots is applied to burns, skin sores, swellings, boils etc. A fibre obtained from the outer stems is used to make cordage, whilst the cottony seed hairs are used as a stuffing material in toys etc or as tinder to start fires.

Oxalis corniculata

Yellow Sorrel is a low-growing annual or short-lived perennial plant, rarely more than 1cm tall but spreading to form clumps 15cm or more across. This is another weed that can become a nuisance if it gets into pot plants, where it spreads rapidly by seed and underground bulbils. Both the leaves and the flowers have a pleasant acid flavour, rather like sorrel. They are very small and fiddly to harvest, but can be added to salads.

The leaves are used as an antidote to poisoning by the seeds of Datura spp, arsenic and mercury, and the leaf juice has a soothing effect when applied to insect bites, burns and skin eruptions.

Plantago major

Common Plantain is a common lawn weed. This perennial plant grows up to 20cm tall, though it will be much lower when growing in a frequently cut lawn. Although most gardeners mercilessly root it out of their lawns, it actually does no harm when growing there and, indeed, helps to maintain the fertility of the lawn. The young leaves are rather bitter and tedious to prepare because the fibrous strands need to be removed before use, but they have been used as a potherb. It is best not to use the leaf stalk since this is even more fibrous than the leaf. They can be blanched in boiling water before using them in salads in order to make them more tender. Although very tedious to harvest, the seed can be ground into a meal and mixed with flour when making bread, cakes etc. The whole seed can also be boiled and used like sago. Common plantain is a safe and effective medicinal herb. The leaves are used externally as a healing poultice and treatment for bleeding, quickly staunching blood flow and encouraging the repair of damaged tissue. Internally, they are used in the treatment of a wide range of complaints including diarrhoea, gastritis, peptic ulcers, irritable bowel syndrome, haemorrhage, haemorrhoids, cystitis, bronchitis, catarrh, sinusitis, asthma and hay fever. Plantain seed husks are an excellent treatment for digestive disorders. They contain up to 30% mucilage that swells up in the gut, acting as a bulk laxative and soothing irritated membranes.

Polygonum aviculare

Knotweed is an annual plant growing to 30cm in height. It is a common and invasive weed of cultivated ground, spreading by seed but quite easily controlled. It is an important food plant for the caterpillars of many species of butterflies and also produces an abundance of seeds that are a favourite food for many species of birds. Young leaves and plants can be used as a potherb; they are a very rich source of zinc. The seed, which is rather small and fiddly to utilize, can be used in all the ways that buckwheat (Fagopyrum esculentum) is used, either whole or dried and ground into a powder for use in pancakes, biscuits and pi ole. Knotweed is a safe and effective astringent and diuretic herb that is used mainly in the treatment of complaints such as bleeding, dysentery and haemorrhoids. It is also taken in the treatment of pulmonary complaints because the silicic acid it contains strengthens connective tissue in the lungs. Recent research has shown that knotweed paste applied internally is a useful medicine in the treatment of bacterial dysentery. The plant yields a blue dye that is not much inferior to indigo, whilst yellow and green dyes can also be obtained.

Polygonum japonicum

Japanese Knotweed is not the sort of plant to encourage or even tolerate in the garden. A perennial growing 2 metres or more tall, it spreads very rapidly at the roots to form dense clumps that smother any other plant growing there. Since its introduction from the East, it has become one of our most pernicious weeds, so vigorous that the roots have even managed to send up shoots through tarmac! However, as with all plants, it is not all bad news. A report on the Natural History Programme of the BBC stated that Japanese knotweed is actually becoming a very valuable habitat for spiders, frogs, grass snakes and many other creatures. Its hollow stems allow a wide variety of insects and other small creatures to overwinter and find hiding places, thus a greater abundance of food is provided for insectivores such as frogs, who are themselves eaten by grass snakes. In areas of north Wales where Japanese knotweed has run rife, it is now the primary habitat for grass snakes. The plant also has several edible uses. The young shoots, which have a mild acid flavour, can be eaten in spring, either cooked in the same way as asparagus or used as a rhubarb substitute in pies, fruit soups, jams etc. The seed can be ground into a powder and used as a flavouring and thickener in soups etc, or can be mixed with cereals when making bread, cakes etc.

Prunella vulgaris

Self Heal is a perennial plant, growing up to 15cm tall and often found as a weed in the lawn. The leaves have a somewhat bitter flavour but can be used in salads, soups, stews etc. The bitterness can be reduced or even removed by washing the leaves prior to use. A cold water infusion of the freshly chopped or dried and powdered leaves is used as a very tasty refreshing beverage. Medicinally, self heal has a long history of folk use, especially in the treatment of wounds, ulcers, sores etc. It was also taken internally as a tea in the treatment of conditions such as fevers, diarrhoea,

Edible Plants

sore mouth and internal bleeding. An olive-green dye can be obtained from the flowers and stems.

Pteridium aquilinum

Bracken is an extremely invasive plant and is a noxious weed. It is one of the most widespread plants in the world, being found in all parts of the globe other than the extreme north and south. A perennial plant, growing about 1.2 metres tall, it spreads freely both by the roots and its dust-like spores that can travel hundreds of miles in the air. The plant has a number of edible uses, with the roots and young shoots being eaten. However, there is also evidence to suggest that regular consumption of the plant could cause cancer, so eating it is not recommended.

There are also many non-edible uses. For example: a glue can be made from the rootstock; the rhizome lathers readily in water and can be used as a soap; the roots have been rubbed into the scalp in order to promote hair growth; the ashes of the plant are rich in potassium and can be used as a fertilizer and also in making glass; the dried ferns produce a very durable thatch and the fibrous remnants from edible roots make a good tinder. In addition, the leaves are used as a packing material for fruit, keeping it fresh and cool without imparting any colour or flavour. They can also be used as a lining for baskets, fruit drying racks etc where they help to repel insects and can also help to prevent rot in the fruits. The dried fronds are very useful in the garden as a mulch for somewhat tender plants. This will keep the soil warmer, protect from wind damage and also keep off some of the rain.

Rumex crispus

Curled Dock is a perennial plant growing about 60cm tall. It is considered to be a serious weed of agriculture but perhaps it should be tolerated as much as possible because it is such a good plant for re-establishing fertility in the soil -its deep roots bring up nutriments that would otherwise be lost whilst its leaves make excellent compost. It is also a very important food plant for the caterpillars of many species of butterfly.

Although rather bitter, the very nutritious leaves have been used in mixed salads, cooked as a potherb or added to soups. Only the very young leaves should be used, preferably before the stems have developed, and even these are likely to be bitter. The inner portion of the stems is also eaten whilst the seed can be used as a pi ole or can be ground into a powder and used as flour for making pancakes etc. When roasted, the seed has been used as a coffee substitute. Curled dock has a long history of domestic herbal use. It is a gentle and safe laxative, less powerful than rhubarb in its action so it is particularly useful in the treatment of mild constipation. The plant has valuable cleansing properties and is useful for treating a wide range of skin problem. All parts of the plant

can be used, though the root is most active medicinally.

Sonchus arvensis

Field Milk Thistle is a common garden weed that has occasionally been cultivated as a food plant -in Indonesia they have even produced improved varieties selected for their edible leaves. A perennial growing up to 1.2 metres tall, it spreads by means of seed and its creeping rootstock. The young leaves have a slightly bitter taste but can be added to salads or cooked like spinach. It might be best, though it is not necessary, to remove the marginal prickles. The mild flavoured stems can be cooked like asparagus or rhubarb, whilst the roasted root is used as a coffee substitute.

Stellaria media

A very common garden weed, chickweed grows, flowers and sets seed all year round. An annual plant growing about 15cm it spreads by means of seeds. It is very easy to control by hoeing and it has many beneficial uses. The young leaves have a mild flavour and can be available all year round if the winter is not too severe. Very nutritious, they can be eaten raw in mixed salads, or cooked to make a very acceptable spinach substitute. The small seed can be ground into a powder and used in making bread or to thicken soups. Chickweed has a very long history of herbal use, being particularly beneficial in the external treatment of any kind of itching skin condition. It has been known to soothe severe itchiness even where all other remedies have failed. When applied as a poultice, it will relieve any kind of roseola and is effective wherever there are fragile superficial veins. An infusion of the fresh or dried herb can be added to the bath water and its emollient property will help to reduce inflammation -in rheumatic joints for example - and encourage tissue repair.

Taraxacum officinale

Dandelions are another of those weeds that is at times cultivated for its edible leaves - indeed there are a number of named varieties that have been developed in Europe. A perennial plant growing up to 40cm tall, it may be perhaps be encouraged in a lawn, but in cultivated beds it tends to provide a hiding place for slugs under the leaves. The plant spreads very freely by means of its light seeds, but is easily controlled by hoeing. The leaves are literally packed full of vitamins and minerals, making this one of the most nutritious leaves you can eat. Unfortunately, they have a rather bitter flavour, though we find a few of the leaves added to a mixed salad to be quite acceptable. The bitter tasting root can also be cooked; some people say they have a turnip-like flavour.

When roasted and ground into a powder, they can be used as a much healthier alternative to coffee. The dandelion is

*56   Plants For A Future: **www.pfaf.org***

a commonly used herbal remedy. It is especially effective and valuable as a diuretic because it contains high levels of potassium salts and therefore can replace the potassium that is lost from the body when diuretics are used. The latex contained in the plant sap can be used to remove corns, warts and verrucae. The latex has a specific action on inflammations of the gall bladder and is also believed to remove stones in the liver.

Tussilago farfara

Coltsfoot has a very aggressive root system and will spread very freely if given half a chance. Indeed, it has been shown that the rhizomes can lay dormant in the soil for many years, finally emerging and resuming growth when the soil is disturbed. All in all, this is not a plant to encourage in the garden unless you choose your site with care or find some means of restraining it such as by planting in a large tub that is buried in the ground. A perennial plant, it grows up to 20cm tall, sending up flowering stems in the spring, with the leaves only appearing after it has finished flowering. This habit has led people in the past to believing that the flowers and the leaves were two different plants. All parts of the plant can be eaten, but most have a rather bitter flavour. The flower buds and young flowers, however, have a pleasant aniseed flavour and add a distinctive aromatic flavour to salads. An effective demulcent and expectorant herb, coltsfoot is one of the most popular European remedies for the treatment of a wide range of chest complaints, soothing coughs and helping to get rid of catarrh. It is widely available in health food shops, often in the form of a candied sweet.

Urtica dioica

If there is one plant that every child learns to recognise, it is the stinging nettle. Just one brush up against the stinging hairs on its leaves is enough to produce a lasting memory! A perennial plant, it grows up to 1.2 metres tall and can form very extensive clumps spreading both at the roots and by seed. Apart from its many uses for humans, this is a superb wildlife plant. It can be a nuisance in cultivated areas, but it should be allowed to grow in out of the way places. Stinging nettles have a huge range of uses, only a few of which are mentioned here. The young leaves can be eaten cooked -although they can sting you when raw, once they are cooked they are perfectly harmless and make one of the most nutrient-rich foods you can eat. Do make sure you use gloves or other protection when harvesting and washing them though! Do not harvest leaves from plants that have started to flower, however, since these can develop gritty particles called cystoliths that act as an irritant to the kidneys. If you cut the plants down twice a year, just before they start to flower, then you will ensure a good supply of fresh young leaves in the summer and will also prevent the clump from becoming too vigorous. Cutting them more than twice a year

will severely weaken them and probably kill them over a period of 2-3 years.

Nettles have a very long history of herbal use and modern research has shown the justification for this. For example, a tea made from the leaves has traditionally been used as a cleansing tonic and blood purifier so the plant is often used in the treatment of hay fever, arthritis, anaemia etc. The roots contain substances that have been shown to have a beneficial effect upon the prostate and it is now used in a very effective formula to treat an enlarged prostate. The fresh leaves of nettles have been rubbed or beaten onto the skin in the treatment of rheumatism etc. This practice, called urtification, causes intense irritation to the skin as it is stung by the nettles. It is believed that this treatment works in two ways. Firstly, it acts as a counter-irritant, bringing more blood to the area to help remove the toxins that cause rheumatism. Secondly, the formic acid from the nettles is believed to have a beneficial effect upon the rheumatic joints.

A strong flax-like fibre obtained from the stems is used for making string, cloth and a good quality paper. The leaves are an excellent addition to the compost heap and can be soaked for 7-21 days in water to make a very nutritious liquid feed for plants. This liquid feed is both insect repellent and a good foliar feed. A hair wash is made from the infused leaves and this is used as a tonic and anti-dandruff treatment. A beautiful and permanent green dye is obtained from a decoction of the leaves and stems.

Edible Plants   **57**

Tussilago farfara COLTSFOOT

Stellaria media CHICKWEED

Polygonum japonicum KNOTWEED

Plantago major COMMON PLANTAIN

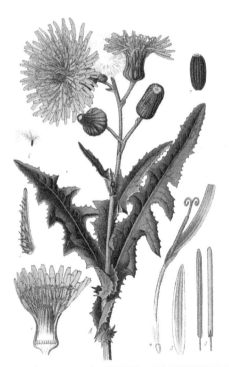
Sonchus arvensis FIELD MILK THISTLE

Pteridium aquilinum BRACKEN

Cirsium species THISTLE

Rumex crispus CURLED DOCK

Polygonum aviculare

58   Plants For A Future: *www.pfaf.org*

Prunella vulgaris SELF HEAL

E. angustifolium WILLOW HERB

Elytrigia repens COUCH GRASS

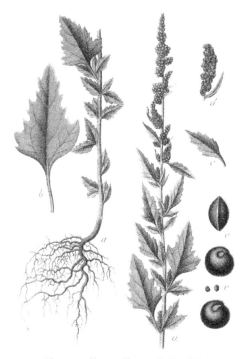
Chenopodium album FAT HEN

C. bursa-pastoris SHEPHERD S PURSE

A. podagraria GROUND ELDER

Oxalis corniculata YELLOW SORREL

Allium vineale CROW GARLIC

Cardamine species BITTERCRESS

Edible Plants **59**

Annuals in the Perennial Garden

Plants For A Future has always focused on providing information about, and encouraged the cultivation and use of, perennial plants. But this does not mean that we discourage the growing of annual plants. This section will look at ways of including many of the conventional annual crops in a perennial garden and will also look at a number of less well-known annuals such as Chinese mallow and pearl lupin. We use the term annual in a rather loose sense to depict those plants we usually cultivate as annual crops (such as runner beans), rather than just limit ourselves to the true annuals that complete their entire life cycle within a year.

Of course, as outlined in the first section of this book, we do not like the idea of growing lots of the same plant in straight lines. Usually the more of any one species that is grown together than the greater the chance of problems with pests and diseases. Thus, if you want to grow annual plants, we recommend integrating them as far as possible with the perennial species. This is not always easy, and there are a number of annual plants that just do not fit easily into a perennial system, but it is surprising how many can do well there.

There are a number of advantages and disadvantages with integrating annuals. The disadvantages include: -

• The plants are more scattered and so harvesting of some crops such as carrots and peas can be more complicated, as you have to wander here and there in order to harvest sufficient quantity.

• You have to be very careful in selecting spots in which to grow the plants, since the perennials around them will often grow rapidly and swamp out the annuals before they can establish themselves.

• It can be hard for the annuals to establish themselves due to the established root systems of the perennials.

• It can be difficult to harvest some crops, especially the larger root crops, since digging them up can disturb the roots of the perennial species.

The advantages include:

• There are a wide range of benefits to the soil and ecosystem

• By scattering your plants amongst the perennials, many problems with pests and diseases can be greatly reduced.

• By selecting complementary growth habits, such as allowing peas to clamber into small shrubs, it is possible to grow more crops in the same area of ground and thus increase overall productivity.

When deciding how to place annuals in the perennial garden, it is important to look at the needs, growth habit and life cycle of each species. The vast majority of cultivated annual food plants are best adapted for growing in sunny situations (many of them such as cabbages, beet and carrots were originally sea-shore plants) Therefore, when selecting a position to grow them amongst annuals you usually need to focus upon the sunnier spots. Very poor results will be obtained if they are grown in the shade, though there are exceptions to this rule that will be noted when dealing with individual species. You also need to take into account the likely size of the annuals you are growing and the perennials that will surround them.

Some plants, such as onions, are very narrow and can fit into smaller places, whilst others such as broccoli are much more spreading and will need quite a bit of space.

We have found that annuals can generally be grown using one of the following methods: ¬

1. Aggressive self-sowers. If allowed to flower and set seed, several annual crops, such as spinach beet and land cress, are more than capable of maintaining themselves year by year so long as they have some bare soil in which their seeds can germinate.

2. Sowing in situ each year. Crops such as radish, peas, onion sets and turnips germinate rapidly and grow sufficiently fast that they can be sown directly into suitable gaps between the perennials.

3. Sowing in pots. Many crops, such as French beans, tomatoes, sweet corn and lettuce can be started off in pots or trays in the greenhouse and then planted out into the garden when sufficiently large.

A few crops, particularly carrots, are quite difficult and labour intensive to grow and/or harvest in an annual garden. They germinate quite slowly, dislike transplanting, and generally do not compete well with the perennials.

We will now look in more detail at the different methods of growing the annuals and which plants fit into which categories. The more conventional food crops will be mentioned in their respective categories, but will not be looked at in detail since more information on these plants can easily be found in conventional gardening books. However, we will look in more detail at those plants that are not so well known as food crops. In all cases we will try to give approximate likely sizes of the plants (height and width) to help you to work out where to place the plants. Please note, sizes are based on how large you are likely to let the plants grow before harvesting them rather than the ultimate size of the plant. Thus where plants are usually harvested and removed before going to seed the size given will be based on size at harvest rather than at flowering.

60 *Plants For A Future: **www.pfaf.org***

Group 1 - the aggressive self-sowers

These are plants that, once established, are generally able to maintain themselves for a number of years by self-sowing. Establishment usually takes the form of simply sowing the seeds in selected spots in the garden. There are two factors in particular that you need to take into account. Firstly, you need to allow at least some of the plants to flower and set seed -in general always allow at least three plants to do this, selecting the three best plants where possible to try and ensure good quality plants in future generations. Secondly, the seed will need some bare earth in which to germinate - usually simply hoeing small areas amongst the perennials is sufficient for this.

The seed is sown in situ. Firstly, you select suitable spaces amongst the perennials - since most seed sowing takes place in the spring you do need a certain amount of imagination to try and picture just how large the perennials are likely to grow over the following months and make sure the spaces you have selected are large enough. The soil is prepared by hoeing it to make a good tilth and then sowing the seed. Even in wet seasons it is necessary to make sure that the soil remains moist enough for the seed to germinate since the ground around perennials can be much drier than in a conventional vegetable garden. In drier seasons it is often wise to wet the soil thoroughly before sowing the seed and also to cover it with something like a sheet of newspaper for a few days after sowing to ensure the moisture remains in the soil. Do not leave it covered for too long, however, since many seeds require light for germination.

There are many interesting and useful plants that will self-sow and look after themselves very well, though not many of these are the better known conventional crops - this is at least partly due to the fact that these have actually been selectively bred over many centuries and have lost the vitality that allows many annuals to become weeds in the garden. In addition, where growing named varieties, it is important to remember that there is a very strong chance the future generations will not breed true since pollinating insects will not mind spreading the pollen around with any wild forms of the plant or other named varieties growing nearby.

The best known vegetable in this section is spinach beet, Beta vulgaris cicla (90cm x 40cm). This is a very productive plant that self-sows very easily and is very worthy of a place in the garden.

Atriplex hortensis.

(180cm x 30cm) Orach is another of those plants with a long history of cultivation, though it is rarely used as a food nowadays. The leaves can be cooked and used like spinach, they have a bland flavour and are traditionally mixed with sorrel leaves in order to modify the acidity of the latter. There are some very ornamental varieties available with bronze or deep red leaves that do not look at all out of place in the flower border - the flavour of these is virtually the same as green leaved forms and they also tend to breed true, so it is possible to use these as self-sowing food crops.

Barbarea verna.

(30cm x 25cm) The leaves of land cress have a hot, spicy watercress flavour that makes a delicious addition to mixed salads. Once this plant is established in your garden it will usually self-sow quite freely and is able to germinate and thrive even in quite strong weed competition; it will even grow in a lawn. In mild climates you may be able to pick leaves all the year round, in colder climates the plant is likely to die down during the winter but will be back very quickly in the spring.

Chenopodium album.

(90cm x 20cm) Most gardeners are more likely to think of fat hen as a weed rather than as a food crop, but this plant does have a long history of use as a food. Indeed, there is at least one named variety - called Magenta , it is considered by some people to be one of the very best tasting of all potherbs. If you grow Magenta it is important to remember that it will almost certainly not breed true but will cross with the wild form to produce a mixture of seedlings. Since fat hen is such a common weed, you do not usually have to work at establishing it in your garden -it will usually turn up with or without an invitation! Once it is there, you can use it in a number of ways. The leaves make a very acceptable spinach substitute - the taste is a little bland but this can be improved by adding a few stronger-flavoured leaves. The young flowering heads can be harvested and cooked in the same way as broccoli - they make a very tasty alternative to that plant. The seed is also edible and very nutritious. It is rather small and the easiest way of utilizing it is to ground it into a flour and add it to conventional wheat flour when making cakes, bread etc. The seed does need to be soaked for 12 hours in water beforehand in order to leech out a bitter substance found on the outside of the seed (you can use this water as a hair wash, or spray it over plants to act as a bird deterrent).

Claytonia species.

(15cm x 15cm) Miner s lettuce, C. perfoliata, and pink purslane, C. sibirica, are low growing plants that, once established, will usually self-sow with abandon. It is easy enough to control, though, and is very unlikely to become a problem. Both of these plants are very shade tolerant and are some of the few plants in this book that will do well in

Edible Plants **61**

dense shade. They are also very useful in that they supply their edible leaves throughout the year, even in the depths of winter. Many people would find the leaves of pink purslane a bit too earthy to enjoy, but miner s lettuce is milder and more enjoyable. Both can be used in salads and can also be cooked, though they then have a somewhat slimy texture.

Eruca vesicaria sativa.

(60cm x 25cm) The strongly flavoured leaves of rocket have become quite a popular salad ingredient. There is a perennial species with a very similar and probably superior flavour. to the annual species. The annual version can provide salad leaves for much of the year in the milder parts of the country where seeds will germinate and grow all year round. In colder areas it is possible to harvest leaves from mid spring to late autumn.

Papaver somniferum.

(60cm x 20cm) Surprisingly few people know that the opium poppy is also grown as a food crop, yet this is the plant that those delicious little blue seeds come that are used as a topping on bread and rolls. Opium poppies are also commonly grown as an ornamental crop for their delicate flowers (in the British climate yields of the drug opium from the sap of the plant are so low that it is perfectly legal to grow the plant). This is an excellent plant to grow amongst the annuals. When growing the plant for its seed, allow the seed capsules to dry on the plant before harvesting the whole capsule and tipping the seed out. You may then want to tip some of the seed onto the garden for next year s crop.

Valerianella species

(30cm x 20cm). There are two different species of this genus that make excellent salad plants, V. locusta, corn salad, and V. eriocarpa Italian corn salad. The seeds of these plants are more commonly sown in late summer in order to provide mild-flavoured leaves for the salad bowl throughout the winter.

When allowing the plants to self-sow, most germination is likely to take place in the spring and summer and so will not be as suitable as a winter crop. If this happens to you then it would be a good idea to harvest some of the seed and sow it yourself in late summer.

Group 2 - Plants that can be sown in situ.

The method of establishing the plants here is exactly the same as for the self-sowers mentioned earlier, with the exception that you have to do it every year since the plants are no vigorous enough to maintain themselves by self-sowing See the section on the self-sowers for general information or sowing the seed.

The main requirements here are that the seed is able to germinate rapidly after being sown and that the growth o the young plant is vigorous enough to establish the plan amongst the perennials. There are lots of conventiona vegetables that fit into this category, as well as severa interesting but less well known plants.

The well-known species are the onions and shallots (use onion sets if growing in situ, onion seed will need to be sown in pots), Allium cepa (30cm x 15cm); then there are the many forms of Brassica oleracea such as the cabbage (30cm x 30cm) kale (80cm x 50cm), broccoli (90cm x 60cm), cauliflowe (75cm x 50cm), Brussels sprouts (120cm x 30cm) and Koh rabi (45cm x 25cm); Brassica napus napobrassica, the swed (60cm x 30cm); the many forms of Brassica rapa including turnips (30cm x 20cm) and Chinese cabbages (40cm x 25cm) the forms of Beta vulgaris including beetroot (35cm x 20cm and Swiss chard (40cm x 30cm); then there is perhaps th easiest of all annual crops the radish, Raphanus sativus 20cn x 10cm); Spinacia oleracea Spinach (30cm x 20cm); and th broad bean, Vicia faba (100cm x 20cm). In addition, potat tubers, Solanum tuberosum (70cm x 30cm), can also b planted in situ.

Chenopodium quinoa.

(150cm x 25cm) Quinoa has long been cultivated in S. America as a cereal crop and it is now being more widely grown in other regions of the world as a trouble-free, productive anc highly nutritious food. The seed is unusual amongst plan foods in that it is a complete protein with the same biologica value as milk (most plant proteins are lacking in certain essential amino acids and need to be combined in orde to provide a complete protein). The seed germinates ver quickly and plants grow away rapidly. If the right varietie are chosen, yields in Britain can be very good. Ken Fern go a good yield from the cultivar Dave though he noted tha in wet seasons the dense seed heads can retain moisture anc cause the seed to rot. In such a situation it is better to grov lower yielding varieties such as Temuco or Faro , whicl have more open flower heads.

Chrysanthemum coronarium.

(60cm x 60cm) Chop-suey greens are commonly grown as a food crop in the Orient, whilst being more seen as an ornamental plant in Britain. The young shoots and stems have a strongly aromatic flavour and are rather an acquired taste, though many people are fond of them. They can be cooked as a potherb (do not overcook or they will turn bitter) or the young leaves can be added to mixed salads. Start harvesting the plant when it is about 4 - 5 weeks old and harvest it quite severely to increase productivity and keep the plant smaller. This is a plant that will self-sow successfully in some gardens so, if you grow it and allow it to flower keep a look out for any seedlings in subsequent years.

Fagopyrum esculentum.

(150cm x 30cm) Buckwheat is often cultivated for its edible seeds, but it also provides very nutritious leaves. Although the flavour of these leaves is not really wonderful, they are an excellent source of rutin, a nutrient that has been shown to have a very beneficial effect upon blood circulation. Perhaps the best way to eat them is to either add a few young leaves to a mixed salad or to cook older leaves in a mixture with other leaves such as spinach or cabbage. The seed has a nutty flavour, though it has a somewhat gritty texture. It can be used as a cereal and is often made into foods such as pancakes and noodles.

Malva verticillata.

(150cm x 50cm) Chinese mallow is a truly excellent salad plant with large mild flavoured tender leaves. A very productive and easily harvested crop, plants with leaves 30cm across can still be good to eat. They make a tasty alternative to the lettuce. This plant is supposed to be a bit tender in Britain, but specimens have been seen to thrive on a north facing slope at 150 metres above sea level in Shropshire. Where possible, try to obtain the cultivar Crispa which has more ornamental leaves and a better flavour.

Pisum sativum.

(60cm or more x 30cm) The garden pea is a very well known vegetable, but I have included it here because of its growth habit. Whilst there are dwarf cultivars growing only 60cm or so tall, it is also possible to obtain some of the older much taller varieties that will climb into other plants and support themselves by means of their tendrils. It is well worth getting hold of one of these old varieties and allowing it to scramble its way into a shrub or even a hedge. Yields will tend to be a bit lower, but there will be none of the work involved in providing supports for the plant and some consider that the flavour of some of these old varieties of peas has never been

matched by the newer dwarf forms. An added benefit of growing peas in this way is that when the plants are removed (cut them off at ground level and leave the roots) then as the roots rot they will provide nearby plants with a good supply of nitrogen to promote their growth.

Portulaca oleracea.

(25cm x 25cm). There are two forms of purslane, one with green leaves and a cultivated form with yellow/golden leaves. Both of them make very acceptable salad plants. Growing rapidly from seed, it can be ready for harvesting when only 6 weeks old. A frost-tender plant, it is grown as an annual in Britain but, where the climate suits it better, it can become an invasive weed, spreading freely by means of its seed. The leaves have a somewhat sour flavour, when young they make a delicious addition to mixed salads. Older leaves are best cooked and used as a potherb - they are rather mucilaginous and have been used as a substitute for okra for thickening soups. Purslane leaves, unlike most leaves, are a reasonable source of omega-3 fatty acids, though seed sources such as walnuts are many times richer. The seed is also edible, although it is rather small and fiddly to utilize.

Traditionally, it was ground into a powder and mixed with cereals for use in gruels, bread, pancakes etc.

Tragopogon porrifolius.

(60cm x 30cm) Salsify is occasionally cultivated in the garden

for its edible roots, if allowed to flower then it is also quite an ornamental plant. The flavour of the root is mild and sweet, and is said to resemble oysters. Young roots can be grated and eaten raw in salads, whilst older roots are best cooked. The young shoots, harvested shortly after coming through the ground in spring, are also edible, either raw or cooked, and have a sweet taste.

Group 3 - Plants that are sown in pots

Although it takes more time, and consumes more resources, sowing the seed in pots and growing the plants on for a few weeks is probably the most successful way of integrating annual crops into a perennial garden. The deeper 9cm pots are preferable to the smallest thumb pots, since they allow good root formation before planting out. Sow a few seeds in each pot and then thin either to one plant or a few depending on species (cabbages for example are best thinned to one plant whilst seed crops such as amaranth do well thinned to about three). Plants are put out into the garden once they have a good root system, and must be watered in well to encourage rapid establishment. In dry seasons it might be necessary to water once more.

The majority of annual crops respond well to this method. The main exception is certain root crops such as carrots that really dislike root disturbance and do not grow so well in amongst the perennials.

In addition to all the vegetables mentioned in previous sections, the following conventional crops can also be grown in this way:- Allium cepa, the onion (30cm x 15cm) and Allium porrum the leek 40cm x 15cm); celery (60cm x 25cm) and celeriac (60cm x 25cm), which are both forms of Apium graveolens; endive, Cichorium endiva; (40cm x 25cm) chicory, Cichorium intybus (40cm x 25cm); lettuce Lactuca sativa (30cm x 25cm); tomatoes, Lycopersicon esculentum (150cm x 30cm); parsley, Petroselinum crispum (40cm x 25cm); French beans, Phaseolus vulgaris (50cm x 25cm); and finally, sweet corn, Zea mays (150cm x 30cm).

Amaranthus species.

The amaranths are very fast growing plants that can provide very nutritious leaves and seeds. Several members of the genus have a long history of cultivation as food crops, especially in S. America and some other areas of the Tropics. They are frost tender plants, which is why it is better to sow them in pots in the spring and then plant them out after the last expected frosts. In warmer climates than Britain it would be possible to sow them in situ. The plants grow best in fertile soil - make sure they are well fed whilst in their pots and apply some compost to the soil when you plant them out and they will repay you with an excellent crop of leaves that you can use as spinach, plus a good crop of small seeds that are very nutritious and an excellent source of protein. Whilst all members of this genus can be eaten, the ones especially recommended are:- A. caudatus, a frequently grown ornamental plant known as love lies bleeding (200cm x 45cm)); A. cruentus, the purple amaranth (200cm x 45cm); A. hybridus, rough pigweed (60cm x 30cm); A. hypochondriacus, prince's feather (120cm x 50cm); and A. viridis, calalu (50cm x 40cm).

Anthriscus cerefolium

(30cm x 25cm) The leaves of chervil have a mild aromatic flavour that is suggestive of aniseed. They can be available all year round and make a nice addition to mixed salads, and can also be used as a flavouring in cooked foods such as soups and stews. They form the basis of the seasoning 'fines herbes' and are an essential ingredient of 'bouquet garni'. The leaves should always be used fresh because the delicate flavour does not withstand drying or prolonged cooking. This is a plant that needs to be sown every few weeks during the growing season in order to ensure a continuous supply

of leaves. The earliest sowings can be made in late winter with the final sowing taking place in mid autumn. Whilst the spring, autumn and winter crops are best in a sunny position, the summer crop will do better if given some shade.

Campanula rapunculus

(50cm x 30cm) Rampion was at one time a popular root crop but fell out of favour due mainly to its low yields. This is rather a since the root has a very nice sweet flavour, which some people say is reminiscent of walnuts. They can be eaten both eaten raw and cooked, perhaps grated into salads or cooked with a mixture of other roots such as carrots. The leaves can also be eaten raw or cooked - they have a fairly bland flavour, with a hint of sweetness and are quite acceptable in salads. This is a very attractive plant if you allow it to flower, which it will do in its second year because it is a biennial.

Cucumis sativus

(200cm x 50cm) At first sight, you would not really think of growing cucumbers amongst the perennials, but it can work well. The trick is to treat it as a climbing plant and place it near a shrub that it can grow into. Make sure it is a sturdy shrub, because the weight of the cucumber plant and its fruit is quite considerable and would quite likely break the branches of weaker growing shrubs.

Cucurbita pepo

(100cm x 120cm) Here we are talking about the bush forms of marrow and courgette, not the vigorous trailing types of pumpkin that can send out shoots 5 metres or more in length. Even these bush forms are rather large to fit among the perennials, but there are times when a gap this large is available, either when a new bed of perennials is just being established and large gaps have been left for the new plants to expand into, or in the unfortunate event that a plant has died and left a big hole behind.

Helianthus annuus

(300cm x 30cm) Sunflowers are tall, stately plants, but they have quite a narrow growth habit and take up surprisingly little space on the ground. Commonly cultivated for their edible seeds, they really need a hotter and drier summer than is usual in Britain in order to develop and ripen their seeds without rotting. When started off early in pots, however, they will usually ripen their seeds successfully in most parts of Britain. The oil-rich seeds have a delicious nutty flavour and can be eaten raw or cooked - the oil is often extracted and is commonly used in cooking, as a salad dressing etc. There are several lower growing cultivars of sunflowers that are easier

64   Plants For A Future: www.pfaf.org

to grow in Britain, but make sure it is a form with larger seeds since several of these dwarf forms have seeds that are too small to be of much use.

Lens culinaris

(45cm x 25cm.) It is not widely known that lentils are quite hardy plants that can succeed outdoors at least in the warmer areas of Britain. Although yields per plant are quite low, the seed is a very nutritious and easily digested protein-rich food. They are used in a variety of cooked dishes, they can be dried ground into a flour and added to wheat when making bread etc, or they can be sprouted and used in salads.

Lupinus species

When talking about lupins, most people will think of the stately flowering plants so often seen in the flower border. However, there are a number of species that have been cultivated for their protein-rich seeds which can be used in any of the ways that soya beans are used. These seeds often have a bitter flavour that needs to be removed by soaking them in water for 12 hours, the water being discarded before cooking them. The three species most commonly cultivated as food crops are L. albus, the white lupin (120cm x 25cm); L. angustifolius, the blue lupin (100cm x 25cm); and L. mutabilis, the pearl lupin (150cm x 25cm). There are several named varieties, including some that have much reduced levels of the bitter substances.

Phaseolus coccineus

(200cm x 100cm) Runner beans are quite large vigorous climbing plants, but you can grow them successfully in the perennial garden if you allow them to scramble into taller shrubs or a hedge. Since you are likely to be harvesting the seedpods on an almost daily basis in the summer, do make sure you pick a spot that is easily accessible and does not require you to go trampling all over your other plants to get at them.

Physalis species

(90cm x 80cm) There are two closely related species of tomatillo, P. ixocarpa and P. philadelphica. They both produce an edible fruit that is wrapped up in a papery husk. Related to tomatoes, it can be a delicious replacement for that fruit in cooked dishes such as stews. The fruit can also be eaten raw, but it needs to be very ripe, and even then it is not the type of fruit that many people would like to eat in quantity.

Solanum scabrum / S. lanceifolium

(60cm x 30cm). Looking very similar to our native black nightshade, S. nigrum, the garden huckleberry has been selectively bred to produce an edible fruit which can be cooked and used in preserves, jams and pies. A pleasant musky taste, a few may be eaten raw, though only the fully ripe fruits should be used since the unripe fruits contain small amounts of the toxin solanine (which is also found in potatoes).

Group 4 - The pains in the butt

These are the plants that, for various reasons, Ken Fern categorised as too difficult to fit into a perennial garden, or where particular care needed to be taken. This was because the sheer size of the plants in question is likely to swamp the perennials, or they are slow to germinate and grow. Each plant will be discussed below.

Arctium lappa

(200cm x 100cm) Whilst burdock is thought of mainly as a wild plant and occasional garden weed in Britain, it is a commonly cultivated food crop in Japan where a number of named varieties have been developed. Tolerant of some shade, this large plant needs to be grown where there is plenty of room for it if you are going to let it flower and set seed (it can be up to 2 metres tall and 1 metre wide) and there is a risk that it will swamp any smaller plants nearby. If growing amongst perennials, it really needs to be amongst shrubs. Burdock's edible root is quite thin but long and so you also have to take into account being able to dig in the soil to get the root up. The root can be eaten raw when it is very young, but it is more usual to let it grow larger and then cook it. The flavour is mild and it has the ability, like potatoes, to absorb the flavour of other foods it is cooked with. Burdock is a very healthy food, indeed it is also used as a medicinal herb because of its ability to help clear the body of toxins. A clear case of food being a medicine and medicine being a food!

Chaerophyllum bulbosum

(30cm x 30cm). Turnip-rooted chervil has occasionally been cultivated for its edible root. It is a very easily cultivated plant, once the seed has germinated and herein lies the problem. The seed can be very slow to germinate and really needs to be sown in the autumn as soon as it is ripe. Older seed may take 12 months to germinate. The plant is also rather intolerant of root disturbance so needs to be planted out as

Edible Plants **65**

soon as possible. This is a plant that might be able to self-sow and maintain itself in the garden - allow at least a few plants to flower and scatter their seeds and keep a sharp eye open for seedlings when weeding the garden. But after all this trouble, is the plant worth it? Well, the root is fairly small so overall yields are not high, but it has an excellent aromatic flavour and can be eaten either raw or cooked. When raw it is quite starchy, but becomes sweet and has a floury texture when cooked.

Cucurbita species

(100cm x 500cm) Pumpkins and squashes are very vigorous plants and, since their shoots can be 6 metres or more long, they are much too large to be able to fit into your average flower bed. For those who have the space, it would be worthwhile experimenting with growing them on the sunny side of a shrubbery or even on the south or southwest edge of woodland. Here these climbing plants (for that is what they are in the wild) will spread out over the ground and clamber up into any surrounding plants that they can get a hold of.

Daucus carota sativus

(30cm x 30cm). There are several problems with growing carrots amongst perennials. Firstly, the seed is quite slow to germinate, then the seedlings are frail and slow growing at first. These problems can be easily overcome by sowing the seed in pots as per the previous section - unfortunately the seedlings are very intolerant of root disturbance and plants will not develop good quality roots if they are disturbed. And growing them in 9cm pots does not work since the roots have reached the bottom of the pot before the tops are large enough to plant out - this results in poor quality deformed roots. You could sow the seed in deeper pots, but this is very wasteful of resources, and you soon begin to wonder if it is worthwhile.

Pastinaca sativa

(50cm x 25cm). Parsnip seed is even slower to germinate than carrot seed and, with regard to inclusion in a perennial plants scheme, parsnip suffers from the same problems as carrot (see above).

Conclusion

There are many annuals that fit in quite easily amongst perennial plants and growing them in this way can be a very productive and sustainable use of the land. In addition, you will usually find a considerable drop in the amount of damage caused to plants by pests and diseases - even if some plants get attacked, it is very likely that others will escape completely simply because they are isolated from the attacked plants.

There are also several annual crops that do not fit so well into a perennial system, and rather than worrying about these difficulties, perhaps it is better to find acceptable substitutes from amongst the thousands of perennial plants that have been overlooked as food sources.

Fagopyrum esculentum BUCKWHEAT

Helianthus annuus SUNFLOWER

Cucumis sativus CUCUMBER

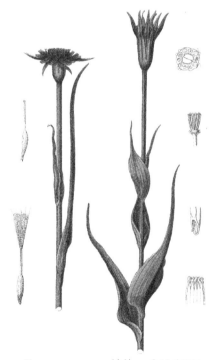
Tragopogon porrifolius SALSIFY

Anthriscus cerefolium CHERVIL

Campanula rapunculus RAMPION

C. coronarium CHOP-SUEY GREENS

Papaver somniferum OPIUM POPPY

Portulaca oleracea PURSLANE

Edible Plants **67**

Amaranthus species

Pisum sativum GARDEN PEA

Lens culinaris LENTILS

Lupinus species LUPINS

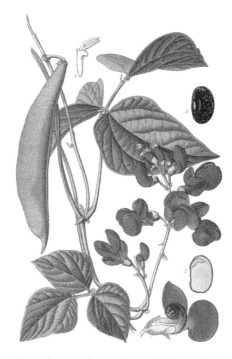
Phaseolus coccineus RUNNER BEANS

Eruca vesicaria sativa

Atriplex hortensis

Barbarea verna LAND CRESS

Cucurbita species

Arctium lappa BURDOCK

C. bulbosum TURNIP CHERVIL

Daucus carota sativus CARROT

Pastinaca sativa PARSNIP

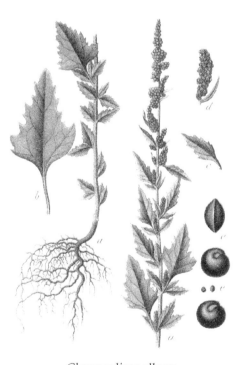
Chenopodium album

Claytonia species

Edible Plants **69**

Index

A

Acca sellowiana see Feijoa sellowiana
Actinidia species 9
Aegopodium podagraria 53
Agastache foeniculum 5, 21
Alexanders see Smyrnium olusatrum
Alfalfa see Medicago sativa
Alliaria petiolata 34
Allium species 21, 28, 34
Allium vineale 53
Almond see Prunus species
Althaea officinalis 43
Amaranths see Amaranthus species
Amaranthus species 64
Amelanchier species 9
American Persimmon see Diospyros virginiana
Anise Hyssop see Agastache foeniculum
Anthriscus cerefolium 64
Apios americana 15
Apricot see Prunus species
Aquilegia vulgaris 28
Araucaria araucana 6, 39
Arbutus unedo 10
Arctium lappa 65
Arrowhead see Sagittaria species
Asclepias tuberosa 29
Asphodeline lutea 29
Atriplex halimus 22, 35
Atriplex hortensis 61

B

Barbarea verna 61
Barbarea vulgaris 35
Barberry see Berberis species
Beans , Runner Beans see Phaseolus coccineus
Beckmannia eruciformis 40
Beech see Fagus sylvatica
Berberis species 10
Beta vulgaris cicla 35
Bittercress see Cardamine species
Blackberries see Rubus species
Bracken see Pteridium aquilinum
Brassica oleracea 22
Breadroot see Psoralea esculenta
Brussels sprouts see Brassica oleracea
Buckwheat see Fagopyrum esculentum
Bunias orientalis 22
Burdock see Arctium lappa

C

Cabbage see Brassica oleracea
Camassia quamash 15
Camellia species 43
Campanula poscharskyana 23, 35
Campanula rapunculus 64
Campanula species 22, 29
Campanula versicolor 5, 22, 35
Capsella bursa-pastoris 53
Caragana species 41
Cardamine hirsuta 35
Cardamine species 54
Carrots see Daucus carota sativus
Castanea sativa 40
Cauliflower see Brassica oleracea
Cephalotaxus harringtonia 40, 43

Cercis siliquastrum 29
Chaerophyllum bulbosum 65
Chenopodium album 54, 61
Chenopodium quinoa 6, 62
Cherry see Prunus species
Chervil see Anthriscus cerefolium
Chervil, Turnip-rooted see Chaerophyllum bulbosum
Chestnut see Castanea sativa
Chichory see Cichorium intybus
Chickweed see Stellaria media
Chicory see Cichorium intybus
Chinese Artichokes see Stachys affinis
Chinese Mallow see Malva verticillata
Chives see Allium species
Chop-suey Greens see Chrysanthemum coronarium
Chrysanthemum coronarium 63
Cichorium intybus 35
Cirsium species 54
Claytonia perfoliata see Montia perfoliata
Claytonia sibirica see Montia sibirica
Claytonia species 62
Claytonia virginica 35
Cogswellia cous see Lomatium cous
Coltsfoot see Tussilago farfara
Columbine see Aquilegia vulgaris
Common Plantain see Plantago major
Corn salad see Valerianella locusta
Cornelian cherry see Cornus species
Cornus sanguinea 43
Cornus species 10
Corylus avellana 43
Couch grass see Elytrigia repens
Courgette see Cucurbita pepo
Crataegus schraderana see Crataegus tournefortii
Crataegus species 5, 10
Crataegus tournefortii 5
Crow Garlic see Allium vineale
Cucumbers see Cucumis sativus
Cucumis sativus 64
Cucurbita pepo 64
Cucurbita species 66
Curled Dock see Rumex crispus
Current, Golden see Ribes odoratum
Cyperus esculentus 5, 15

D

Daffodil Garlic see Allium species
Dandelion see Taraxacum officinale
Date Plum see Diospyros lotus
Daucus carota sativus 66
Daylilies see Hemerocallis species
Desmanthus illinoensis 41
Dioscorea batatas 5, 16
Diospyros lotus 11
Diospyros species 11
Diospyros virginiana 11
Dog s Tooth Violet see Erythronium species
Dogwood see Cornus sanguinea
Duck Potato see Sagittaria species

E

Earth Pea see Lathyrus tuberosus
Elaeagnus species 5, 11
Elderberry see Sambucus nigra
Elytrigia repens 54
Epilobium angustifolium 54
Eruca vesicaria sativa 62
Erythronium species 16

F

Fagopyrum esculentum 63
Fagus sylvatica 43
Fat Hen see Chenopodium album
Feijoa sellowiana (Acca sellowiana) 29
Field Milk Thistle see Sonchus arvensis
Foeniculum vulgare 35
French Sorrel see Rumex scutatus
Fuchsia species 11

G

Garlic Chives see Allium species
Garlic Cress see Peltaria alliacea
Garlic see Allium species
Gaultheria shallon 11
Ginkgo biloba 6
Glaucium flavum 44
Glyceria fluitans 40
Goldenberry see Physalis peruviana
Grape see Vitis vinifera
Ground Elder see Aegopodium podagraria
Ground Nut see Apios americana

H

Hairy Bittercress see Cardamine hirsuta
Hawthorns see Crataegus species
Hazel see Corylus avellana
Hedge garlic see Alliaria petiolata
Helianthus annuus 64
Helianthus tuberosus 16
Hemerocallis species 29
Hibiscus syriacus 23, 30
Hippophae salicifolia 11
Holm Oak see Quercus ilex
Hovenia dulcis 5

I

Indian Potato see Orogenia linearifolia
Iron Cross Plant see Oxalis deppei

J

Japanese Dogwood see Cornus species
Japanese Knotweed see Polygonum japonicum
Japanese Lacquer tree see Rhus verniciflua
Japanese Raisin Tree see Hovenia dulcis
Japanese Wineberry see Rubus species
Jerusalem Artichokes see Helianthus tuberosus
Judas Tree see Cercis siliquastrum
Juglans regia 39, 44

K

Kale see Brassica oleracea
Kiwi Fruit see Actinidia species
Knotweed see Polygonum aviculare

L

Lathyrus tuberosus 5, 16
Leek see Allium species
Lens culinaris 65
Lentils see Lens culinaris
Lilium lancifolium 16
Lime Tree see Tilia cordata

70 Plants For A Future: *www.pfaf.org*

Loganberries see Rubus species
Lomatium cous (Cogswellia cous) 16
Lupins see Lupinus species
Lupinus mutabilis 6
Lupinus species 6, 65

M

Maidenhair Tree see Ginkgo biloba
Mallow see Malva verticillata Crispa
Malva moschata 23, 30
Malva verticillata 5, 63
Malva verticillata Crispa 5
Manna grass see Glyceria fluitans
Marshmallow see Althaea officinalis
Medicago sativa 41
Milkweeds see Asclepias tuberosa
Miner s Lettuce see Montia perfoliata
Monkey Puzzle see Araucaria araucana
Montia perfoliata (Claytonia perfoliata) 23
Montia sibirica (Claytonia sibirica) 35
Morus nigra 11
Musk Mallow see Malva moschata
Myrrhis odorata 24, 36
Myrtus ugni (Ugni molinae) 11

N

Nasturtium see Tropaeolum majus
Nepalese Raspberry see Rubus species

O

Oca see Oxalis tuberosa
Onion see Allium species
Orach see Atriplex hortensis
Orogenia linearifolia 17
Oxalis corniculata 55
Oxalis deppei 5, 24, 30
Oxalis tuberosa 5, 17

P

Papaver somniferum 62
Parsnip see Pastinaca sativa
Pastinaca sativa 66
Pea shrub see Caragana species
Pea, Garden see Pisum sativum
Pea, Tuberous see Lathyrus tuberosus
Peach see Prunus species
Peltaria alliacea 24, 36
Perideridia gairdneri 17
Persimmon see Diospyros species
Phaseolus coccineus 65
Physalis ixocarpa 5
Physalis peruviana 12
Physalis philadelphica see Physalis ixocarpa
Physalis species 65
Pink Purslane see Claytonia species
Pink Purslane see Montia sibirica
Pisum sativum 63
Plantago major 55
Pleurisy Root see Asclepias tuberosa
Plum see Prunus species
Polygonum aviculare 55
Polygonum japonicum 55
Polymnia edulis (Smallanthus sonchifolius) 17
Poppy, Horned see Glaucium flavum
Poppy, Opium see Papaver somniferum
Portulaca oleracea 63

Prunella vulgaris 55
Prunus species 44
Psoralea esculenta 17
Pteridium aquilinum 56
Pumpkins see Cucurbita species
Purslane see Portulaca oleracea

Q

Quamash see Camassia quamash
Quercus ilex 40
Quinoa see Chenopodium quinoa

R

Ramanas Rose see Rosa rugosa
Rampion see Campanula rapunculus
Raspberries see Rubus species
Reedmace see Typha
Reichardia picroides 24, 36
Rhus verniciflua (Toxicodendron vernicifluum) 44
Ribes odoratum 30
Rocket see Eruca vesicaria sativa
Rosa rugosa 12
Rose of Sharon see Hibiscus syriacus
Rosebay Willow Herb see Epilobium angustifolium
Rubus species 12
Rumex acetosa 24, 36
Rumex alpinus 36
Rumex crispus 56
Rumex scutatus 24

S

Sagittaria species 17
Salad burnet see Sanguisorba minor
Salt Bush see Atriplex halimus
Sambucus nigra 30
Sanguisorba minor 36
Self Heal see Prunella vulgaris
Shallon see Gaultheria shallon
Shepherd s Purse see Capsella bursa-pastoris
Siberian pea shrub see Caragana species
Sium sisarum 18
Skirrett see Sium sisarum
Smallanthus sonchifolius see Polymnia edulis
Smyrnium olusatrum 36
Solanum lanceifolium see Solanum scabrum
Solanum scabrum (S. lanceifolium) 65
Sonchus arvensis 56
Sorrel see Rumex acetosa
Spinach Beet see Beta vulgaris cicla
Squashes see Cucurbita species
Stachys affinis 18
Stellaria media 56
Stinging Nettle see Urtica dioica
Sunberries see Rubus species
Sunflowers see Helianthus annuus
Sweet Chestnut see Castanea sativa
Sweet Cicely see Myrrhis odorata
Sweet Violet see Viola odorata

T

Tara Vine see Actinidia species
Taraxacum officinale 24, 36, 56
Taxus baccata 12
The Black Mulberry see Morus nigra
The Strawberry Tree see Arbutus unedo
Thistle see Cirsium species

Thyme see Thymus vulgaris
Thymus vulgaris 36
Tiger Lily see Lilium lancifolium
Tiger Nuts see Cyperus esculentus
Tilia cordata 25
Tomatillo see Physalis
Torreya nucifera 40
Toxicodendron vernicifluum see Rhus verniciflua
Tragopogon porrifolius 63
Tree Collards see Brassica oleracea
Triticum aestivum 41
Tropaeolum majus 31
Tropaeolum tuberosum 18
Turkish Rocket see Bunias orientalis
Tussilago farfara 57
Typha angustifolia 31
Typha latifolia 18

U

Ugni molinae see Myrtus ugni
Urtica dioica 25, 57

V

Valerianella locusta 36
Valerianella species 62
Viola odorata 31, 36
Vitis vinifera 44

W

Walnuts see Juglans regia
Welsh Onion see Allium species
Wheat see Triticum aestivum
Willow-Leaved Sea Buckthorn see Hippophae salici-folia

Y

Yacon see Polymnia edulis
Yam see Dioscorea batatas
Yampa see Perideridia gairdneri
Yellow Asphodel see Asphodeline lutea
Yellow Sorrel see Oxalis corniculata
Yew see Taxus baccata
Yucca baccat 31

Edible Plants   71

EDIBLE PLANTS

There are over 20,000 species of edible plants in the world, yet fewer than 20 species now provide 90% of our food. However, there are hundreds of less well-known edible plants from all around the world that are both delicious and nutritious.

It is our belief that plants can provide us with the majority of their needs, and in a way that cares for the planet s health. A wide range of plants can be grown to produce all our food needs and many other commodities, whilst also providing a diversity of habitats for the native flora and fauna.

This book describes and provides advice on growing some of the lesser known and unusual edible plants, with an emphasis on perennials.

An inspirational guide to choosing and growing unusual edible plants

Made in the USA
Monee, IL
11 November 2022

17564851R00044